Japanese Language Teaching

Japanese Language Teaching
A Communicative Approach

Alessandro G. Benati

continuum

Continuum International Publishing Group

The Tower Building   80 Maiden Lane, Suite 704
11 York Road   New York
London SE1 7NX   NY 10038

British Library Cataloguing-in-Publication Data
A catalogue record for this book is available from the British Library.

ISBN: 978-0-8264-9881-6 (Hardback)
       978-0-8264-9882-3 (Paperback)

Library of Congress Cataloging-in-Publication Data
The Publisher has applied for CIP data.

Typeset by Newgen Imaging Systems Pvt Ltd, Chennai, India
Printed and bound in Great Britain by MPG Books, Cornwall

In memory of my mother
Anna Maria Ferrari

Contents

Acknowledgements

First of all I would like to thank Bill Van Patten and James Lee for their support and encouragement over the years. What I have learned about second language acquisition and language teaching I very much own to them.

I would also like to express my gratitude to all the Japanese postgraduate students in the Masters in Language Learning and Japanese Language Teaching at the University of Greenwich for helping me to reflect on many issues regarding the teaching of Japanese and assisting me in developing tasks and activities which I hope can be used for teaching Japanese more communicatively. I am also very grateful to the Institute of International Studies in London and the Japanese Foundation for allowing me to consult their libraries. A special thank to Mr. Zushi for his continuous support.

I also own a special thank to Noriko Hikima, Kuri Komatsu and Sami for providing priceless advice, help and suggestions on developing Japanese language activities/tasks.

I would also like to express my gratitude to the School of Humanities and the University for having supported my work since I joined this institution. Last but not least a big thank you to Bernadette, Grace and Francesco for their moral support and encouragement during my work.

Finally I would like to thank all the staff at Continuum for their help in the production of this book. I particularly would like to thank Janet, Guardeep and Colleen.

Abbreviations

ALM	Audio-lingual methodology
CLT	Communicative language teaching
CR	Consciousness raising
EI	Explicit instruction
L1	First language
L2	Second language
MOI	Meaning-output instruction
PI	Processing Instruction
SIA	Structured input activities
SLA	Second language acquisition
TI	Traditional instruction

Introduction

Japanese Language Teaching: A Communicative Approach is a text-book written in order to help students, instructors and young researchers reflect on certain topics related to second language learning and communicative language teaching. The text-book is designed for those undergraduate students or trainee teachers with little or no knowledge of theory and research in second language learning and communicative language teaching. On one hand, this book seeks to explore some issues related to language learning which could be considered to have underpinned the communicative language teaching approach. On the other hand, it provides suggestions for good communicative classroom tasks in the teaching of Japanese. Japanese teaching practice has mainly concentrated on teaching the grammatical system of the language and providing learners with very little opportunities to develop communicative skills. In my view, the teaching of Japanese to second language learners in the United Kingdom is still very traditional and this is also proved by the use of traditional books used by teachers to teach Japanese. This text-book is an attempt to reflect on why, what and how the communicative language teaching approach should be incorporated into the teaching of Japanese. At the same time, its main purpose is to encourage students, instructors and young researchers to undertake empirical studies of Japanese language acquisition and teaching to further their understanding of Japanese second language acquisition.

This text-book provides the reader with the underpinning knowledge to analyse some of the main issues around the role of grammar instruction and communicative language teaching and to relate these issues to his own experience so that he can apply them in his own practice as an instructor, researcher or material developer. The book has the following aims:

(1) to review studies and relevant theory in second language acquisition to prove a theoretical and empirical underpinning for a more communicative approach to Japanese language teaching;

(2) to provide an overview of research investigating the role of a focus on form component in language acquisition in order to reflect on the role of instructional interventions in Japanese language teaching;

(3) to develop an understanding of the vital role of input in second language acquisition and draw some conclusions on how we can provide better input for second language learners of Japanese;

(4) to provide an overview of research measuring the effects of different grammar instruction approaches in order to provide guidelines to language instructors in the design of Japanese grammar tasks;

(5) to provide Japanese language instructors with an overview of how the theoretical principles can be applied for designing and preparing communicative activities in the teaching of Japanese language;

(6) to galvanize readers to synthesize the material so that they themselves can design a series of activities in Japanese which can be used in an upcoming class period with their students and serve as a springboard for discussion in language teaching methodology;

(7) to provide the underpinning knowledge in second language research methodology and in particular the experimental method, to enable readers to carry out experimental research in this field.

In order to achieve its aims the book is structured into three different parts.

In Part A of this book our purpose is three-fold: to briefly review key research findings in second language acquisition focusing particularly on the role of input, interaction, output and formal instruction; to review some of the research carried out in the acquisition of Japanese as a foreign language, which supports main theories in second language acquisition; to review some of the research which investigated the role of focus on form, including research on the acquisition of Japanese, and present some of the implications for language teaching.

In Part B, the main characteristics of the communicative approach will be presented and examined with the intention of suggesting effective ways to develop grammar tasks and communicative tasks in teaching Japanese.

Different approaches to grammar instruction will be reviewed in order to provide samples for grammar tasks in the teaching of Japanese. In particular, the focus is on the use of input enhancement techniques and structured input activities which are all very effective communicative approaches used to incorporate the teaching of grammar in a communicative framework of language teaching.

Implementation of communicative language teaching in the teaching of Japanese is be explored by reflecting on how to develop listening comprehension activities, oral exchange information tasks, role-plays, reading and writing communicative tasks.

In Part C of the book an introduction to the process of conducting classroom research through the use of an experimental methodology is given. Examples will be provided on classroom-based research into the acquisition of Japanese. The final chapter is dedicated to the presentation of the results of an experimental study measuring the effects of an alternative approach to teaching grammar on the acquisition of two features of the Japanese linguistic system.

This text-book has two main purposes. First, to provide the tools for making Japanese language teaching more communicative. Second, to provide the instruments to conduct more research into the teaching and learning of Japanese. I hope we have achieved our two main goals.

Part A
Preliminary Considerations

In Chapter 1, we review some of the theories and classroom-based research findings that have been conducted to investigate the role of important constructs and factors in SLA (e.g. input, interaction, output, role of instruction). The main implications for the teaching of these theories and research findings will be highlighted in the attempt to support and justify a more communicative approach to the teaching of Japanese.

In Chapter 2, the role of instruction is explored in more detail by reviewing the major developments in research on the effects of focus on form in SLA. The question is not whether or not an instructional component makes a difference in SLA, but rather whether there is a type of intervention that is more effective than another at promoting SLA.

Preliminary Considerations

Chapter Outline

Introduction

One of the purposes of second language acquisition (SLA) research is to understand how people learn a second language. Among the scope of SLA research is the desire to answer questions such as: What factors affect acquisition?, What is the role of input in SLA?, What is the role of output in SLA?, What is the impact of formal instruction? Van Patten (1999) has distinguished between SLA and instructed SLA. He defines SLA as a field of enquiry that 'concerns the study of how learners develop an internal linguistic system'. He describes instructed SLA as a field of enquiry that 'focuses on the extent to which the development of the learner's internal linguistic system can be effected by instructional efforts'.

Overall SLA research has mainly focused on the acquisition of English and romance languages such as French, Spanish and Italian. However, the acquisition of Japanese by foreign learners has been the focus of attention of recent research (Kanno, 1999; Otha, 2001a). In this chapter, we briefly review theory and research in SLA which includes studies on the acquisition of Japanese as a second language (L2) in the following three areas: studies investigating the role of input, interaction and output; studies measuring the effects of positive and negative evidence; studies investigating the effects of formal instruction. Our objective is to reflect on the main findings of these studies and to be able to make some generalizations from theory and research which will provide us with a better understanding of the nature of SLA and at the same time offer instructors some practical indications on how to make the teaching of Japanese as an L2 more effective and communicative.

Behaviourism and the innate position: preparing the path for communicative language teaching

As argued by Omaggio Hadley (2001:43), 'recent reviews of language acquisition theory have attempted to group various theoretical perspectives along a kind of continuum, ranging from *empiricist views* on one end to *rationalist* or *mentalist* positions on the other.' According to the rationalist position, humans possess an internal grammar that constraints the acquisition of a second language (Chomsky, 1965). This view is in strong opposition to the behaviourist theory. As outlined by Van Patten and Williams (2007:18) behaviourism 'attempts to explain behaviour without reference to mental events or internal processes. Rather, all behaviour is explained solely with reference to external factors in the environment'. At the heart of behaviourism is the belief that language learning is a process which consists of acquiring verbal habits by imitating and repeating good habits. For behaviourists, language was seen as a progressive accumulation of correct habits and the main objective of instruction was to ensure that learners made no errors during language production. Behaviourists thought that the first language (L1) could be the cause of errors as learners transfer the habits of their L1 into the learning of the L2 (negative transfer). The pedagogical and practical implications of the behaviourist theory were the so-called Audio-lingual method (ALM). The ALM is an inductive and structural approach to language teaching based on mechanical and pattern language practice. The practice in the ALM consisted of a type of exercise called 'drills practice' (repetition and substitution/transformation drills). L2 learners have to repeat, manipulate or transform a particular form or structure in order to complete a task (examples of this practice will be presented in Chapter 3). In the ALM, learners were able to complete a task without being involved in any communicative practice as, according to behaviourists, producing the target language too prematurely would have induced L2 learners to make errors and acquire bad habits (see Box 1.1 which indicates the main characteristics of the ALM).

Box 1.1 Audio-lingual methodology: implications for teaching

(1) Learners were encouraged to learn the L2 inductively.
(2) Learners were exposed to the target language at all time.
(3) Learners follow a very structural syllabus focus on structure and form rather than meaning.
(4) Learners were exposed to correct models/patterns of the target L2.
(5) Learners were asked to listen and to repeat.
(6) Learners were engaged in mechanical practice (drills).
(7) Learners were corrected for inaccurate imitations.
(8) Learners must become accurate in the target L2. Linguistic competence is the main goal of instruction.

One of the most important contributions to the development of a communicative approach to language teaching was Chomsky's criticism of behaviourism. Chomsky (1975) criticized the view that L2 language learning is a process of mechanical habit formation as language learning cannot be considered just as imitation and repetition. According to Chomsky, a child possesses a knowledge of language universals (Universal Grammar) and generates from that knowledge a series of hypotheses about the particular L1 that the child is learning. These hypotheses are modified and corrected in the light of the input that the child is exposed to. Chomsky sees L1 acquisition as characterized by two main factors: an internal mechanism (language acquisition device) that is innate and the input that children are exposed to in their environment. The presence of an innate hypothesis-making device in the child emphasizes clearly the active role played by the language learner. This is clearly in antithesis to the behaviourist view and the ALM. In the ALM approach, the teacher plays a crucial instructional role in managing the learning process and determining the type of language practice. For Chomsky, learners have their own internal syllabus to follow and the role of the teacher is reduced from structuring the learning path to presenting the 'linguistic data' which the student reacts to and manipulates in order to internalize a set of rules.

The classroom experimental study conducted by Savignon (1972) also undermined the behaviourist view of language acquisition. Savignon's study was the first empirically based research to compare ALM versus communicative language teaching (CLT). The population of this study consisted of three groups learning French in a College where they were studying French four days a week followed by one day laboratory practice. The three groups received the same ALM treatment during the four training days (1 hour a day), but instruction differed on the laboratory practice day (1 hour). The first group received an extra hour of ALM training; the second group received one hour of cultural studies practice; the third group was exposed to communicative practice. All groups were tested (communicative and standardized proficiency tests) at the end of the instructional treatment and the results showed that the 'communicative group' was overall superior to the other two groups on the communicative competence tests designed by Savignon and performed equally to the other groups on the other standard tests of proficiency (listening and reading tests). The results of Savignon's study indicated that communicative language ability develops as learners engage in communication and not as result of mechanical drill practice.

Wong and Van Patten (2003) have also criticized ALM and drills practice. Overall, the results of the empirical evidence reviewed by Wong and Van Patten (2003) have clearly indicated that drills practice is not an effective tool for learning an L2. A growing body of evidence in romance and non-romance languages (see Chapter 2) has shown that mechanical and traditional practice does not foster acquisition. Lee and Benati (2007a) have conducted a classroom study measuring traditional and non-traditional approaches to grammar instruction in the acquisition of Japanese, in which they have provided evidence which shows that drills and mechanical practice are not an effective practice in language teaching and are not responsible for learners improved performance. In their study, they compared a group of adults receiving traditional instruction (TI) that included paradigmatic explanation of the targeted linguistics features which was followed by mechanical drills practice, to a second group of adult learners of Japanese exposed to a different approach of grammar instruction called processing instruction (PI) on the acquisition of Japanese past tense forms (such as *ikimashita*) and affirmative vs. negative present tense forms (*ikimasu* vs. *ikimasen*). Lee and Benati (2007a) showed that paradigmatic explanation of grammatical rules followed by mechanical drill practice does not have a positive effect on acquisition. Learners receiving this type of instruction did not show any substantial improvement in their performance. Lee and Benati (2007a) concluded that TI that contains mechanical practice is not an effective approach to language learning and does not promote acquisition.

Another scholar who openly challenged behaviourism was Pit Corder (1981). He maintained that we should allow learners to produce errors rather than correcting them. In this way, we can study them systematically. According to Corder, errors are a priceless source to understand learner's behaviour and L2 learners' cognitive development. Corder (1981) affirmed the importance of the use of language in real situations to perform authentic communicative functions and he recommended an approach to language teaching where L2 learners are given these opportunities.

Question to reflect on . . .

Has the behaviourist theory/audio-lingual method influenced the way Japanese is taught? Do text-books in Japanese contain drill practice/activities?

The ALM was criticized as a method of language teaching for a series of reasons. First of all, it does not take into consideration cognitive processes involved in the acquisition of an L2. Second, it is a very mechanical and repetitive method based on the wrong assumption that practising and memorizing correct patterns of the target language is sufficient for learning that language. Finally, it is a method that does not stimulate and motivate L2 learners.

Language acquisition is a more complex phenomenon than the one described by behaviourism. It is a phenomenon in which both internal (innate and internal mechanism) and external factors (input, interaction and output) interact and play an important role in the acquisition of an L2. It is by understanding these mechanisms and the role of external factors and why they occur, that we can make our language teaching methodology more effective and we can facilitate the acquisition of another language.

Input and output in second language acquisition

Input and input processing

Many scholars (Gass, 1997; Caroll, 2001; Van Patten, 2004) have agreed that input is a necessary and vital factor for the acquisition of a L2. Acquisition is seen by these scholars as the development of an implicit, unconscious system. Gass (1997:1) considers input a key variable in SLA and has argued that 'no model of second language acquisition does not avail itself of input in trying to explain how learners can create second language grammar'.

Sharwood-Smith (1986:252) sustained that 'input has dual relevance for the learner: interpretation involves processing for meaning and processing for competence change.' The different ways in which L2 learners might process input might have different consequences. In the first scenario, L2 learners are exposed to the input and they might process input for meaning in order to cope with communication demands. In the second scenario, L2 learners' process input for acquisition as input might trigger a change in learner's interlanguage, and learners might be able to convert the input into intake (Sharwood-Smith, 1993).

Input provides the primary linguistic data for the creation of an implicit unconscious linguistic system. When learners receive input they are feeding their developing system with the data it needs to start the process of acquisition (Van Patten, 1996).

Gass (1988, 1997) has developed a SLA model which goes from input to output and where both input and output play a role. In this model he argues that not all the language data available to L2 learners is noticed. As pointed out by Gass (1988:202) 'a bit of language is noticed in some way by the learner because of the saliency of some particular features'. However, Gass (1997) has argued that not all input becomes intake and learners are not always able to store the grammatical information about the target language into their developing system. L2 learners may need further input. In the final stage of Gass's model, learners have access to output to produce the target language.

Van Patten's model (1996, 2002, 2004) shares some common characteristics to the model put forward by Gass (1988). Van Patten's model of acquisition is characterized by three main phases as depicted in Figure 1.1 (Van Patten, 1996:41).

Process 1   Process 2   Process 3

INPUT → INTAKE → DEVELOPING SYSTEM → OUTPUT

Process 1 = input processing

Process 2 = accommodation and restructuring

Process 3 = access and production strategies

Figure 1.1 Input processing model.

According to Van Patten (1996) only a small portion of the input that L2 learners are exposed to is processed. This is due to learner's processing limitations (process 1) and processing problems (see the following chapter for a description and discussion of Van Patten's processing principles). The portion of input processed is called intake (it is what learners have perceived and processed in the input through their internal processors). The second stage of the Van Patten SLA model (process 2) involves a series of processes for incorporation of intake into the developing system. These processes are called 'accommodation' and 'restructuring'. Accomodation is the process of accepting a form or structure into the developing system after learners have mapped that form or structure with a particular meaning during the first phase. Restructuring is the process of integrating the new form or structure into learner's developing system which will cause a change in that system. The final stage in this model (process 3) consists of a set of processes (access and production strategies) that acts on the acquired L2 system and determines what is available at a given time for productive use.

In Van Patten's model, only part of the input is passed through intake into the developing system and eventually into output by the learner. Changing the way L2 learners process input and enriching their intake might have an effect on the developing system that subsequently should have an impact on how learners produce the L2. Input processing is concerned with those psycholinguistics strategies and mechanisms by which learners derive intake from input. In Van Patten's theory, when learners attend or notice input and comprehend the message, a form–meaning connection is made. Developing the ability in L2 learners to map one form to one meaning is essential for acquisition. Form refers to surface features of language (e.g. verbal and nominal morphology, words) and functional items of language (e.g. prepositions, articles, pronouns). Meaning refers to referential real-world meaning. Form–meaning connections are the relationship between referential meaning and the way it is encoded linguistically.

Question to reflect on . . .

Can you think of few examples of a form–meaning connection learners of Japanese must make in the input they receive?

When learners hear the following sentence in Japanese *Kinō italia ni ikimashita* (Yesterday, I went to Italy) and understand that -*mashita* means that the action is in the past, a form–meaning connections is made. Input processing is the process that converts input into intake. When learners attend to input and are able to make efficient and correct form–meaning connections, then that input becomes intake.

One experimental study in the acquisition of Japanese that provides supporting evidence for the input processing model is the one conducted by Lee and Benati (2007b). In this study, the two researchers measured whether learners' ability to process input can be enhanced through structured input activities (SIA). The main scope of SIA is to alter the way L2 learners process input and to facilitate the ability for learners to process correct form–meaning connections. The main purpose of their study was to compare the relative effects of a group receiving SIA with a different group exposed to enhanced SIA on the acquisition of Japanese past tense verb morphology. Lee and Benati (2007b) showed that structured input practice with or without enhancement was an effective grammar practice and was responsible for learners improved performance.

In relation to the input processing model, this demonstrated that SIA was successful at helping learners process sentences containing the Japanese grammatical form -*mashita* and consequently, having positive effects on their developing system see Box 1.2 on the overall teaching implications for the input processing theoretical model).

Box 1.2   Input Processing: practical implications for teaching

(1) Grammar instruction must take into consideration how L2 learners process input.

(2) Grammar instruction should provide opportunities to make accurate and efficient form–meaning connections.
(3) Grammar tasks should be structured to force L2 learners to attend to a form and connect it with its meaning.
(4) Grammar instruction should keep in mind that acquisition is intake dependent.

Comprehensible input and interaction

Behaviourism argued that acquisition can be fostered through input manipulation (mechanical practice) and provision of corrective feedback (error correction). This view does not take into account of learners' active processing (internal factors) and there is no support or empirical evidence for this position in SLA research.

Krashen (1982) has underscored the role of comprehensible input in SLA. According to Krashen, in order for input to be an effective tool for acquisition, it must contain a message that must be comprehended by L2 learners. For Krashen (1982), acquisition requires first and foremost exposure to comprehensible input. Krashen's input hypothesis (1982) maintains that input becomes comprehensible as result of simplifications with the help of contextual and extra linguistics clues. As a result of this view, he has hypothesized (Krashen Monitor Theory, 1982) that if learners are exposed to enough comprehensible input and are provided with opportunities to focus on meaning rather than grammatical forms, they are able to acquire the L2 in a fashion similar to their acquiring L1. Krashen (1982) has proposed a five-hypotheses model:

(1) the acquisition-learning hypothesis;
(2) the natural order hypothesis;
(3) the monitor hypothesis;
(4) the input hypothesis;
(5) the affective filter hypothesis.

To briefly summarize the five hypotheses we can say that according to Krashen we can develop two systems that are independent. The 'acquisition system' (unconscious and implicit) is activated when we are engaged in communication, whereas the 'learning system' (conscious and explicit) functions as a monitor and corrector of our production. As said before, according to this theoretical model, grammatical features are acquired in a specific order and errors are testimony of natural developments. It is paramount that learners are exposed to input (comprehensible) and learn an L2 in a very relaxed environment which enhances their motivation and does not pressurize them. This is a theory that has obvious pedagogical implications (see implications for language teaching in Box 1.3) and was translated into an approach to language teaching called the Natural Approach.

Box 1.3   Krashen monitor theory: implications for teaching

(1) L2 teaching should focus on providing a rich variety of comprehensible input. This can be achieved with the help of linguistics and nonlinguistics means.
(2) L2 teaching should provide learners with opportunities to use language spontaneously and meaningfully.
(3) L2 teaching should provide learners with opportunities to focus on meaning and message rather than grammatical forms and accuracy.
(4) L2 teaching should engage learners in listening and reading activities first. There should be no immediate pressure to produce the target language.
(5) L2 teaching should be interesting and create an environment that enhances motivation in L2 learners and avoid that learners can become anxious.

Van Patten (2003:25) defines input as 'the language that a learner hears (or reads) has some kind of communicative intent'. Input is the main ingredient for the acquisition of a second language. As outlined by Lee and Van Patten (1995:37) two main characteristics make input useful for the learner:

(1) input must be meaning-bearing;
(2) input must be comprehensible.

First of all, in order to be effective input must contain a message that learners must attend to. Second, and more importantly, input has to be easily comprehended by the learner if acquisition is to happen. These two characteristics are explained if we keep in mind that acquisition consists of the building up of form–meaning connections in the learner's head (Ellis, N. 2002; Van Patten, 2004). Features in language (e.g. vocabulary, grammar, pronunciation etc.) make their way into the learner's language system only if they are linked to some kind of meaning and are comprehensible to L2 learners. However, not all the input, even if it is comprehensible and meaningful, is picked up by learners.

Learners use copying strategies to derive intake from input (some of these processes will be examined in Chapter 2).

The role of comprehensible input and interaction in SLA has been the focus of research not only in English and other European languages (see Gass and Selinker, 2001), but it has also been investigated in Japanese. The effects of comprehensible input have been particularly the focus of a classroom study in the acquisition of Japanese. Nakakubo (1997) compared two groups of intermediate Japanese learners. The first group was provided with simplified input in listening comprehension tests and the second group received unmodified input. The results of this study showed that the first group outperformed the second group in the listening comprehension test used to measure learner's performance. This study re-emphasized the importance of providing L2 learners of Japanese with comprehensible and simplified input in the language classroom.

In the interaction hypothesis (see Gass, 1997; Van Patten and Williams, 2007), input is seen as a significant element/factor for acquisition without which Learners cannot acquire an L2. Ellis (1994) distinguishes two types of input: interactional and non-interactional. In the case of interactional input (see also Long, 1980; Pica, 1983), he refers to input received during interaction where there is some kind of communicative exchange involving the learner and at least another person (e.g. conversation, classroom interactions). In the case of non-interactional input, he refers to the kind of input that occurs in the context of non-reciprocal discourse, and learners are not part of an interaction (e.g. announcements). In the former case, learners have the advantage of being able to negotiate meaning and make some conversational adjustments. This means that conversation and interaction make linguistics features salient to the learner. Many scholars (Mackey, 1995; Long, 1996; Gass, 1997) have indicated that conversational interaction and negotiation can facilitate acquisition (Interaction hypothesis, Long, 1980). Learners sometimes request clarifications or repetitions if they do not understand the input they receive. In the attempt to facilitate acquisition, one person can request the other to modify his/her utterances or the person modifies his/her own utterances to be understood. Among the techniques used for modifying interaction the most common are:

(1) clarification request (e.g. what did you say?);
(2) confirmation checks (e.g. did you say . . ..);
(3) comprehension checks (e.g. do you understand?).

Input, interaction, feedback and output are the main components of the interaction hypothesis (see main implications for teaching in Box 1.4).

Box 1.4   Interaction theory: implications for teaching

(1) L2 instructors must give L2 learners the opportunities to communicate and interact with each other.
(2) L2 instructors must engage L2 learners in negotiating meaning.
(3) L2 instructors need to give L2 learners opportunities to communicate.
(4) L2 instructors must provide L2 learners with opportunities to participate in planned and unplanned discourse. The discourse should contain many samples of the linguistic features that learners are trying to learn.

Loschky (1994) carried out a study to investigate the effects of comprehensible input and interaction on vocabulary retention and comprehension. English native speakers learning two locative expressions of Japanese were the subjects of this study. Three groups were formed: unmodified input, premodified input, and negotiated input. The task involved non-native speakers of Japanese to follow spoken description given by native speakers of Japanese. The results showed that negotiation of meaning had a positive impact on comprehension even though the three groups performed similarly in the sentence verification test and vocabulary test.

Other studies investigating the acquisition of Japanese as a foreign language (Inagaki and Long, 1999; Mito, 1993) have yielded very interesting results showing the importance of conversational interaction in SLA. Otha (2001a) has pointed out that there is overwhelming evidence which shows the benefits of peer L2 interactive tasks in the learning of Japanese. He argued that (2001a: 126) the use of peer interactive tasks in the teaching of Japanese provides learners with the ability to use the L2 for a wide range of functions and activities. He maintained that compared with teacher fronted practice, through interactive tasks learners have more opportunities to help each others to recall and use vocabulary, notice grammatical errors and learn how to interact appropriately. The studies we briefly reviewed in this paragraph seem to corroborate the hypothesis that interactionally modified input is very effective as it facilitates comprehension and L2 learners' development.

The role of output

Krashen (1982) has assigned a limited role to output as according to him it has no function in building L2 learners' developing system. Krashen's view is that input helps learners making form–meaning mappings which are vital for internalizing the grammatical properties of a target language. Swain (1985) has developed a hypothesis called 'the comprehensible output hypothesis' according to which, language production (oral and written) can help learners to generate new knowledge and consolidate or modify their existing knowledge. Swain (1985) assigns several roles for output (see Box 1.5).

Box 1.5   The role of output

(1) Output practice helps learners to improve fluency.
(2) Output practice helps learners to focus on form.
(3) Output practice help learners to check comprehension and linguistic correctness.
(4) Output helps learners to realize that the developing system is faulty and therefore notice a gap in their system.

Swain has pointed out that comprehensible input might not be sufficient to develop native-like grammatical competence and learners also need comprehensible output. Learners needs 'pushed output' that is speech or writing that will force learners to produce language correctly, precisely and appropriately. According to Swain (1995:249) 'producing the language might be the trigger that forces the learner to pay attention to the means of expression needed in order to successfully convey his or her own intended meaning.'

According to Van Patten the ability to produce forms and structures in output does not necessarily mean that forms and structures have been acquired. We need to distinguish between output as interaction with others and output as practice of forms and structures. In Van Patten's view (2003), learners' implicit system develops as learners process the input they receive. Output promotes noticing of linguistic features in the input and conscious awareness of language and language use. It can also provide additional input to learners so that they can consolidate or modify their existing knowledge. In Van Patten's view (2003), the role of output is important (promotes awareness and interaction with other learners), but it does not play a direct role on the creation of the internal linguistic system. Van Patten et al (2004:42) have sustained that 'we have little if any experimental data that clearly show that acquisition is somehow output dependent.'

Van Patten (2003:20) also makes a clear distinction between skill acquisition and the creation of an implicit system. Conscious presentation and manipulation of forms through drills and output practice might help L2 learners to develop certain skills to use certain forms/structures correctly and accurately in controlled tasks but has very little impact on the development of the implicit system responsible for acquisition.

Researchers have carried out a series of studies investigating the role of output in SLA (Pica, 1994; Mackey, 1995). These studies have confirmed the importance of conversational interactions.

Iwashita (1999) has conducted a study with learners of Japanese as a foreign language with a focus on pushed output. One- and two-ways tasks were used to measure the effects of output and interaction between subjects. The results of this study showed that learners can positively use output to interact with each other (clarifications checks and confirmation checks), provide feedback and produce modified output. Learners in this study were also able to modify their output through negotiation of meaning. The main findings were similar to a previous one conducted by Haneda (1996) who investigated the role of pushed output among intermediate learners of Japanese as a foreign language. Nagata's (1998) study provided support for Swain's output hypothesis as she compared two groups of learners of Japanese receiving computer assisted comprehension and production practice. The first group was exposed to an input-focused computer programme which contained explicit grammar instruction and comprehension-based practice. The second group received an output-focused programme with the same explicit grammar instruction component and production activities practice. The main findings from this study showed that the output-based group performed better than the comprehension group in the production of honorifics in Japanese and equally well in the comprehension test for these structures. Encouraging learners to produce the target language, exposes L2 learners to linguistics problems that might lead learners to notice things they do not know (Swain, 1995). Interaction with other speakers might allow learners to notice things in the input that they have not noticed before.

Question to reflect on . . .

What is the role of input and output in SLA? Are both necessary for acquisition to take place? Can you think of one input-based and one output-based task which can be used effectively in Japanese language teaching?

Positive evidence and negative evidence

The interest in the role of positive and negative evidence in SLA is partly related to the fact that exposure to comprehensible input is a necessary ingredient for acquisition but might not be enough. Learners might need some form of instruction to notice and process some forms or structures that might otherwise not be noticed in the input (see following chapter). When learners are acquiring an L2 they have access to two types of evidence: positive and negative. Positive evidence is the various well-presented utterances learners are exposed to in the input. Positive evidence is used to show learners what is possible in a targeted L2. Negative evidence can be provided by the instructors through feedback to L2 learners about the incorrectness of utterances. The debate as to whether and to what extent positive and negative evidence contribute to SLA is still very much an open one. According to the non-interface position (see following paragraph) exposure to positive evidence is solely responsible for the development of L2 learners interlanguage, and negative evidence has very little role.

However, White has argued (1987, 1991) that some forms or structures are more difficult to be acquired through positive evidence alone. This is particularly the case of a structure that is not part of the Universal Grammar. White (1987, 1991) describes a situation where input does not supply L2 learners with all the necessary information (adverb placement in English) and some form of intervention is required. Long (1996) has maintained that negotiation of meaning elicits negative feedback including recasts which in turn can help learners notice a form or structure that otherwise might go unnoticed. As highlighted by Sharwood-Smith (1991) negative feedback might take several forms in conversational interaction which go from puzzled looks, confirmation checks and clarifications requests, to corrective recasts. A variety of studies (among others see Carroll and Swain, 1993; Spada and Lightbown, 1993; Doughty and Verela, 1998) have investigated the beneficial effects of negative feedback and have overall confirmed its positive effects in helping the development of learners' grammatical competence. The way feedback on errors was provided in traditional instruction mainly consisted in explicit error correction. However, a more implicit approach to negative feedback would involve a provision of corrective feedback (drawing learners' attention to errors) within an overall focus on message.

Long argues that (1996) recast is a form of implicit negative feedback where the learner's attention is drawn to mismatches between the input and the output. Recast is a form of corrective feedback where instructors provide a correct version (correct form) of the utterance. Recast enables teachers to provide feedback without hindering L2 learners' communicative intent. One line of research (Lyster and Ranta, 1997) on recast has argued that it is not effective in eliciting immediate revision by learners of their output. A second line is instead more positive about the role of recast (Doughty, 1999).

A study by Koyanagi, Maruishi, Muranos, Ota and Shibata (1994) and also Moroishi, (2001) have supported the view that recast is an effective type of corrective feedback in the case of Japanese conditional forms (*to*, *ba*).

Question to reflect on . . .

Would (in your opinion) recast be an effective way to provide corrective feedback to learners of Japanese? Can you think of an example of different ways of providing negative feedback for learners of Japanese?

Inagaki and Long (1999) have conducted a study investigating the role of recasts in the acquisition of adjective ordering and locative construction in Japanese. Five groups were used in order to measure the relative effects of the recast technique. The authors claim that the findings provide 'some evidence in support of the claim that implicit negative feedback plays a facilitative role in SLA' (Inagaki and Long, 1999:26 and see a review of the effects of recast in the acquisition of Japanese in Ohta, 2001a).

Iwashita (2003) conducted a study which compared the relative effects of different types of implicit corrective feedback (including reaction, clarification requests and confirmation checks) on the acquisition of Japanese -*te*- form of the verb, word order and particle use in locative-initial constructions. She concluded that the effects of implicit feedback will vary depending on the linguistic features in focus. In this study recast was effective in promoting learning of the -*te*- form but not in the case of the other two linguistics forms.

From the studies reviewed on Japanese language acquisition we can argue that learners benefit from both positive and negative evidence. The question is how we can efficiently and effectively provide both in the language classroom. In the following paragraphs and more extensively in Chapter 2 of this book, we will present and review different techniques of focus on form (manly input enhancement and the structure input practice) which attempt to focus learners' attention to formal properties of the target language in the input in order to facilitate acquisitional processes.

The effects of instruction on acquisition

Learning and acquisition

One of the most prominent and at the same time most criticized theories in SLA research has been Krashen's Monitor Theory (Krashen, 1982). Krashen develops his theory out of a series of studies conducted by Dulay and Burt (1974). The so-called 'morpheme order studies' discovered that learners, irrespective of their L1, acquire grammatical items in the same order. Learners seem to follow a natural order in acquiring an L2. There is empirical evidence (Felix, 1981; Lightbown, 1983; Kaplan, 1987) to indicate that L2 learners go through a natural sequential order in acquiring linguistic features, and this natural order is not affected by formal instruction.

Krashen makes a clear distinction between 'learning' and 'acquisition' as they are two independent and unrelated systems. For Krashen acquisition is an unconscious process which does not benefit from any conscious learning. Learning is a conscious process and it is the result of formal instruction (knowledge of the grammatical rules). Learners use this knowledge to monitor their speech. Krashen assigns to formal instruction a very 'fragile and peripheral role' (1993:22). According to Krashen, grammar instruction plays a very limited role in SLA, since he argues that learned knowledge that results from grammatical instruction does not turn into acquisition.

As previously said, Krashen emphasizes the key role of comprehensible input and meaningful input as the main vehicles for acquisition. Instructors should provide meaningful and comprehensible input in the language classroom. There are certain practical implications for classroom practice consistent with Krashen's theory (see Box 1.3). First of all, Krashen advocates that instruction should focus on developing learners' communicative competence (see Chapter 3 in this book) rather than on grammatical perfection. Second, acccording to Krashen, the main function of language teaching is to provide comprehensible input (simplified and modified through the use of various means) in the language classroom. Therefore, most, if not all classroom activities, should be designed to evoke communication and not wasted in grammatical lectures or manipulative exercises and error correction which has a negative effect in terms of learner's motivation and attitude.

The facilitative position

A different view in the role of grammar teaching is the so-called 'facilitative position' that claims that formal instruction seems to be able to speed up the process of natural acquisition. Opponents of Krashen have developed different models of SLA in the belief that 'learned' or 'explicit' knowledge can become 'acquired' or 'implicit' knowledge provided that learners have the opportunity and motivation to automatize new rules through practice. McLaughlin (1978) distinguishes between controlled and automatic processing. According to McLaughlin, learners acquire an L2 when they are able to move from control to automatic processing. Bialystok (1982) has also developed a model of SLA based on two types of knowledge which can interact: explicit knowledge and implicit knowledge. He claims that through practice, explicit turns into implicit. This is also the view of Anderson (1983) who distinguishes two types of knowledge: declarative knowledge (knowing that) and procedural knowledge (knowing how). Anderson indicates that learning begins with declarative knowledge and slowly becomes proceduralized (procedural knowledge is acquired by performing a skill) through practice.

Krashen (1982) has argued that learning and acquisition are not connected and explicit knowledge is quite different from implicit knowledge (non-interface position). In clear opposition to this view, other researchers (DeKeyser, 1995, 2006; Robinson, 1995) have taken a different view arguing that explicit and implicit knowledge are indeed connected, and instruction has a facilitative role. Ellis (Ellis, N. 2002:175) argues that acquisition has an implicit nature and it is the product of 'slow acquisition of form-function mappings and the regularities therein'. Learners need to be provided with opportunities to process forms and make form–meaning connections through grammar instruction so that forms of a target language can become part of their interlanguage system.

Van Patten (2003) has strongly argued that SLA involves the creation of an implicit and unconscious linguistic system. His view is also corroborated by a study (Van Patten and Mandell, 1999), conducted with one of his associates where he demonstrated that L2 learners have an explicit system and develop an explicit knowledge of rules, but it is the implicit system learners are creating in their heads that is ultimately responsible for their fluent performance in the L2. As noted by Van Patten (2003:13) 'L2 learners store the explicit or explicitly learned information separately from their implicit systems.'

Classroom evidence reviewed by Long (1983) who has investigated the effects of grammar instruction has indicated that instruction might have a facilitative role in SLA. More recent reviews (Larsen-Freeman, 1991) have also shown that while grammar instruction has no effects on acquisition sequences, it is of value in promoting rapid and higher levels of acquisition. Norris & Ortega (2000) have conducted a meta-analysis of studies which attempted to measure the effectiveness of grammar instruction. The results of this review indicated that grammar instruction (particularly explicit types of instruction) has a facilitative effect on the rate and ultimate success of acquisition.

SLA research measuring the effects of explicit rule information has provided mixed results. Positive effects for instruction have been measured in grammatical judgement tasks and controlled production tasks as in the case of Robinson (1996, 1997). No positive effects have been found in studies assessing the effects of explicit information as a component of a grammar instruction approach called processing instruction (Van Patten and Oikkenon, 1996).

Classroom research in French immersion programmes (Harley & Swain, 1984; Harley, 1989) has shown that even after years of exposure to comprehensible input learners still can't reach a certain level of accuracy. The findings in these studies have highlighted the inadequacies of approaches to language teaching where the emphasis is only on meaning-based instruction and grammar teaching is not provided. Despite the fact that input is a crucial and vital element in the acquisition process, it may not be sufficient in SLA (see Van Patten and Williams, 2007).

Research on the effects of grammar instruction has suggested that while providing comprehensible input in the classroom is essential, we must at the same time engage learners in communicative tasks where grammar can be enhanced through the use of different techniques. Some kind of focus on grammatical forms might be necessary to help learners develop higher levels of accuracy in the target language.

It is increasingly evident that instruction might have a facilitative role by enabling learners to notice linguistics features in the input and improve their interlanguage. In the so-called 'noticing hypothesis', Schmidt (1990, 1994) has argued that in order to acquire a language it is necessary for learners to pay conscious attention to forms/structures of the targeted language. It is necessary for learners to notice forms in the target input; otherwise learners might just process input for meaning and fail to process and acquire specific linguistic forms. Many features and characteristics of the target language might influence and determine whether learners are able to notice a form in the input (e.g. frequency; perceptual saliency and communicative value of a given form/structure).

Sharwood-Smith (1991) argues that it is not whether grammar should be taught but in what way it should be taught. Sharwood-Smith (1986:274) had claimed that

> instructional strategies which draw the attention of the learner to specifically structural regularities of the language, as distinct from message content, will under certain conditions significantly increase the rate of acquisition over and above the rate expected from learners acquiring the language under natural circumstances.

Sharwood-Smith (1991) takes the argument further, emphasizing that grammar instruction or as he calls it 'consciousness-raising' can take many different forms along two main dimensions: elaborateness and explicitness (explicit or implicit approaches). In the following chapter we will take this further and focus on three different approaches to grammar teaching which seems to be successful at helping L2 learners to notice and process grammatical forms in the input. These different approaches have been supported by some empirical evidence. Sharwood-Smith (1991) has argued that it is important to draw learners' attention to specific features in the input, but it is ultimately the learner who determines what to do with the input. In addition to that, not all the input is internalized and absorbed and becomes intake (Input processing theory). Some factors related to the characteristics of the target language itself (e.g. frequency or saliency of particular forms) might influence the ability for L2 learners to notice forms in the input. There are also internal factors that might be responsible for how learners process language : (influence of L1 (universal grammar theory); processing strategies (input processing theory); readiness (processability theory), see following paragraphs).

Question to reflect on . . .
What is the role of grammar instruction in Japanese language teaching?

Teachability/learnability hypothesis

One of the areas that SLA research has focused its attention on is to investigate interlanguage developments. A series of empirical studies have been conducted to understand development sequences in SLA and as a result of these studies a hypothesis was formulated. This hypothesis called the teachability hypothesis has been defined by Ellis (Ellis, R., 1994:656) as 'the most powerful account we have of how formal instruction relates to learning'. This hypothesis has been advanced by Pienemann (1984) as a result of extensive research into the naturalistic acquisition of L2 German word order rules and L2 English acquisition. The main aim of this research was to investigate whether formal instruction would alter the sequence of acquisition. Pienemann (1984) has advanced a series of hypothesis concerning the effects of instruction on SLA. First of all, he argued that instruction will not enable learners to acquire any developmental features out of sequence. Second, instruction will enable students to acquire developmental features provided that the processing operations required to produce those features that precede it in the acquisitional sequence have already been mastered. Finally, instruction directed at developmental features for which the learner is not ready may interfere with the natural process of acquisition. These hypotheses have been tested in several studies by Pienemann (1984, 1987) which showed that instruction cannot help the learner change the natural order of SLA; however, in Pienemann's view, instruction can promote language acquisition if the interlanguage is close to the point when the structure to be taught is acquired in the natural setting. The teachability hypothesis relies on the possibility that instruction could help the learner to alter the natural route of development, if the learner is psycholinguistically ready. Therefore, according to Pienemann (1984) instruction can facilitate the SLA process if it coincides with when the learner is ready; it can improve the speed of acquisition, the frequency of role application and the different contexts in which the role has to be applied. The processing challenge is that learners must learn to exchange grammatical information across elements of a sentence. In language learning this ability develops gradually and learners will gradually move up the structure (first accessing words, then their syntactic category, then joining them in a phrase). Learners follow a very rigid route in the acquisition of grammatical structures. Structures become learnable only when the previous steps on this acquisitional path have been acquired. Pienemann's conclusions could be summarized as follows: stages of acquisition cannot be skipped; instruction will be beneficial if it focuses on structures tailored to the next developmental stage. Kanagy's (1991, 1994) has undertaken research on interlanguage development in Japanese. In particular, the acquisition order of negation in Japanese has been investigated. The results of this research have shown a clear development sequence for patterns of negation in L2 learners. For example, at stage 1, beginner learners would produce only predicate external negation (*nai* or *nai-desu*) and attached it to verbs or adjectives. At stage 2 learners are able to use various negation forms such as −*masen* and *ja-arimasen*. According to Kanagy (1999:62) learners of Japanese from different L1 follow a similar route of development in learning to express negation. In addition to that, learners follow a specific order of acquisition (V & N > A) of negation for predicate types, and non-past negative constructions are acquired before past tense forms. These results are also confirmed in more recent studies in Japanese (Hansen-Strain, 1993). One of the conclusions from Kanagy's studies (1991, 1994) is that the instructional teaching orders do not seem to match acquisition orders. This is also the case in studies investigating other L2. For example, the third person - *s* - in English is a morpheme taught rather early in most English language programmes, but it is one of the last verb morphemes to be acquired in speech. The acquisition of verb morphemes in English (Lee & Van Patten, 1995) seems to follow an universal pattern (-ing-regular past tense-irregular past tense-third person −s-). Learners seem to follow a particular path (Lightbown, 1983; Pica, 1983) in the way to develop the L2 system regardless of the order in which grammatical features are taught. Overall we have evidence not only in European languages but also in Japanese that instruction does not appear to cause a difference in the acquisition order. Di Biase and Kawaguchi (2002) have successfully attempted to test the typological validity of the processability theory in Japanese (verbal inflection-V-te V- benefactive, causative and passive) which has a different syntactic and morphological structure compared with romance languages.

In his processability theory Pienemann (1998) argues that internal psycho-linguistics factors and processing constraints determined the sequences of acquisition of features in a targeted language. This position is in line with Corder (1967) who suggested that learners follow internal strategies to organize linguistics data, and these strategies are not necessarily affected by outside influences. Pienemann's processing procedures are acquired in the following sequence: word- category- phrase- sentence. If we can take again the case of L2 learners learning Japanese negation we might say for instance that at word level learners would process the overall meaning of the sentence before forms. Once they have recognized the meaning of a word they can assign words to a lexical category and functions. If it is true that learners pass through predictable stages while acquiring the grammatical system of a second language and this is also the case of Japanese SLA, one question we need to address is: what is the role of instruction? (See implications of this theory for language teaching in Box 1.6.)

Box 1.6   Processability theory: implications for teaching

(1) Instructors must take into consideration that learners follow a very rigid route in the acquisition of grammatical structures. It is not a matter of whether or not instruction has a role to play but it is a matter of when. Instruction will be beneficial if it focuses on learnable structures.
(2) Instructors must take into consideration that learners will not be able to produce forms or structures for which they are not psycholinguistically ready.

Kawaguchi (2005) has also provided some evidence for the applicability of the processability theory to the acquisition of Japanese. The data collected by Kawaguchi from learners of Japanese showed that learners follow predictable orders of acquisition (lexical-phrasal-sentence) in SOV order (Japanese is a SOV language as the verb is always in final position).

Question to reflect on . . .

Is there a role for formal instruction in the acquisition of Japanese?

Summary

In this chapter, we have attempted to briefly review some of the theories and the findings of research in SLA with two main objectives. Our main scope was to look at these findings in SLA and determine whether there are some implications for language teaching which can also be applied to the teaching of Japanese.

The role of input has been the main focus of attention in SLA research. Monitor Theory (Krashen, 1982) affirms that input is the necessary ingredient in SLA as learners acquire a second language in a similar way to that in which we acquire our first language. However, the question raised by Van Patten and Williams (2007:9) is whether input is sufficient for acquisition. As it is a fundamental and necessary ingredient in SLA, for (Gass, 1997), input must first contain a message which a learner is supposed to attend to and, second, and more importantly, input has to be easily comprehended by the learner. As proposed by Van Patten (1996, 2004) learners must process input and their internal mechanism must work on the processed input for that implicit system to develop. Learners have to comprehend what the speaker is saying if acquisition is to happen. Features in language (e.g. vocabulary, grammar pronunciation) make their way into the learner's language system only if they are linked to some kind of meaning and are comprehensible to the learner (see Hatch 1983; Lee & Van Patten 1995, 2003). Comprehensible and meaning-bearing input is therefore one important element in SLA. Although we have established that there are limits on the effects of output on SLA, output has clearly a role to play. Interaction with other speakers might allow learners to notice things unnoticed before. Swain (1985) sees negotiation of meaning and opportunities for interaction as paramount for the acquisition of an L2.

The ability to make form–meaning connections is enhanced if the language is structured in such a way that certain features of the language are more salient. Gass (1988, 1997) has emphasized that instruction does in fact prepare the path for acquisition although initially learners do not fully acquire what is taught when it is taught. Instruction should aim at helping learners to pay selective attention to form and form–meaning connections in the input. Whatever approach to grammar teaching we adopt, we should devise grammar activities that facilitate learners in noticing and comprehending linguistics features in the input. Gass (1988) suggests that selective attention is facilitated by devising instructional activities whose main aim is helping learners to interpret the meanings of some specific forms in the input, rather than equipping learners with conscious rules. Van Patten (1996) has argued that SLA involves the creation of an implicit linguistic system outside awareness. Learners are not aware of the properties that govern this system. L2 learners possess an implicit system and sometime intuitively know if a sentence is correct or not but cannot explain why. As previously said, certain features in L2 have to be acquired before others (stages of development), and we know that learners make particular errors as they reach different stages regardless what their L1 is and no matter what kind of formal instruction they receive. In terms of acquisition orders L2 learners acquire various grammatical features in a predetermined order and regardless of their L1 and formal instruction.

In this chapter, we have argued that the effects of instruction are limited. This claim is based on the observation that instruction cannot alter developmental sequences or cause learners to skip stages (Pienemann, 1984). Learners are guided by some internal mechanism in SLA that instruction cannot override (Pienemann, 1998). In addition to that, instructional orders do not match acquisition orders. The order in which learners learn grammatical forms does not necessarily match the way those forms where taught by instructors in the classroom. As highlighted by Van Patten (2003), SLA is a complex phenomena which on one hand consists of the creation of an implicit system by L2 learners and on the other hand, is affected by many factors as it develops (e.g. specific sequence of acquisition and orders of acquisition). Van Patten (2003) has argued that extensive practice on a form has no effects if learners are not ready as learners follow universal developmental sequences in their interlanguage development.

Despite this, grammar instruction has a role to play. There seems to be evidence that instruction might have some kind of facilitative effect, most notably in 'speeding' up acquisition (Ellis, 1994). Therefore, although a substantial body of research has suggested that learners work on an internal schedule which depends on various factors, there is also experimental research which clearly indicates that grammar instruction in SLA is beneficial and has a facilitative function. Learners might learn certain forms more quickly if they receive grammar instruction as they are exposed to richer and more complex input than those in a naturalistic environment where input is limited to conversational language. Grammar instruction can help learners to be aware of things in the input that might be otherwise missed or learners might get wrong (Van Patten, 1996, 2002, 2004). It can help learners to make better form–meaning connections vital for acquisition (Ellis, N., 2002; Van Patten, 2004). Attention to language forms might allow learners to notice some aspects of the linguistics system. In addition grammar instruction could be used to make certain forms in the input more salient so that learners might notice them and perhaps process them more quickly (Sharwood-Smith, 1991). Classroom and textual input might be the source of a possible facilitative effect and instruction may aid in comprehension which in turn enhances chances of acquisition (Van Patten, 1996).

Although, some types of grammar teaching (see following chapter) could be beneficial as they can accelerate acquisition, there seems to be psycholinguistics constraints which determine whether grammar instruction is successful or not (processing problems will be discussed in the following chapter).

The question is: can we draw some implications for Japanese language teaching from the theories and research on the role of formal instruction, input, interaction and output which we have briefly reviewed in this chapter? We must agree with Lee and Van Patten (2003) on the fact that instruction should move from input to output and provide L2 learners with opportunities to reflect on formal properties of the language and at the same time to use the language for communicative purposes through interactive tasks. These are the main implications for Japanese language teaching that teachers of Japanese should take into account which we can be drawn for what we have said in this chapter about some of the findings in SLA:

- Traditional grammar teaching (paradigms followed by mechanical drills) is inadequate and has no direct effects on SLA. Japanese grammar should not be presented and practised in a traditional way.
- Japanese grammar teaching should be meaning-based and tied to input and communication.
- Focus on input should first take into consideration how learners process input.
- Grammar teaching might have a positive effect if targets the way learners process input.
- Learners should be exposed to input that is comprehensible, simplified and meaning bearing.
- Negative evidence (corrective feedback) has a facilitative role.
- Although input is a necessary ingredient and a main factor for acquisition, focus on form should be incorporated in a communicative approach to the teaching of Japanese. This focus on form might allow learners to notice and process particular grammatical properties of the target L2. The question that need to be resolved is what type of focus on form.
- Interactive communicative tasks should be promoted for speech production.
- Learners should be asked to perform interaction tasks where they negotiate meaning.
- Output practice will help learners to notice forms, interact with other learners, expose learners to more input and eventually help learners in the development of skills.
- Production should be meaning–based as whenever learners produce language, the language they produce should be for the purpose of expressing some kind of meaning.

More questions to reflect on . . .

(1) Can you summarize (key concepts) the main SLA theories and findings briefly reviewed in this chapter?
(2) Can you find some more relevant empirical evidence (Japanese studies) in support of some of the theories/findings presented in this first chapter?
(3) Are there any other implications for teaching of Japanese, which have not been outlined in this chapter?

Key terms

Acquisition vs. learning: Krashen makes a clear distinction between learning and acquisition. Learning is a conscious process and it is related to the development of explicit knowledge. Acquisition is a subconscious process and related to the development of an internal and implicit system. In this book we use both terms with the same meaning.

Audio-lingual method: teaching method based on the behaviourist view according to which learning another language is about learning good habits and avoid bad habits. It is a method based on the assumption that learning is enhanced through the use of memorization, grammar manipulation and drill practice.

Developing system: the internal implicit system of L2 learners.

Input: the language L2 learners hear or read. This is the raw material learners are exposed to and process.

Intake: the portion of the input that is filtered and processed by the learner.

Input comprehensible: according to Krashen (1982) input must be modified to make sure that it is comprehended by the learner.

Input meaning-bearing: input is a vehicle for communication. It must carry a message.

Input processing: this theory refers to psycholinguistics (interpretation strategies) constraints in processing form/structure in the input.

Interaction hypothesis: according to this hypothesis learners acquiring language as L2 are encouraged to interact in the target language in order to communicate.

Monitor theory: this refers to the Krashen model of acquisition which emphasizes the importance of the role of input, natural processes and learner's motivation in SLA. The teaching method originated from this theory is called 'The Natural Approach'.

Output: Output can be defined as the the language that L2 learners produce.

Recast: a type of corrective feedback in which we provide a correct version of an utterance.

Teachability/learnability hypothesis: according to this theory specific structures should be taught only when L2 learners are developmentally ready to acquire the specific structure of the language.

Universal Grammar: this is the term used by Chomsky to refer to the innate knowledge that we bring to the task of learning a second language.

Further reading

Doughty, C. and Williams, J. (Eds) (1998). *Focus on Form in Classroom Second Language Acquisition.* Cambridge: CUP.

Ellis, R. (1994). *The Study of Second Language Acquisition.* Oxford: OUP.

Gass, S. M. and Selinker, L. (2001). *Second Language Acquisition: An introductory course.* Rowley, MA: Newbury House.

Mitchell, R. and Miles, F. (2004). *Second Language Learning Theories, 2nd ed.* London: Hodder Arnold.

Ohta, J. (2001a). *Second Language Acquisition Processes in the Classroom: Learning Japannese.* Mahwah, NJ: Lawrence Erlbaum Associates.

Sanz, C. (Ed.) (2005). *Mind and Context in Adult Second Language Acquisition.* Washington, DC: Georgetown University Press.

Van Patten, B. and Williams, J. (Eds) (2007). *Theories in Second Language Acquisition.* Mahwah, NJ: Lawrence Erlbaum Associates.

Van Patten, B. (2003). *From Input to Output: A Teacher's Guide to Second Language Acquisition.* New York: McGraw-Hill.

The Role of Focus on Form

Chapter Outline

Introduction: focus on form and focus on forms

In the previous chapter we established that there is evidence, including evidence on L2 learners learning Japanese, showing that L2 learners follow developmental sequences (see Pienemann, 1998), learn morphemes in a similar order, might have access to innate knowledge (see White, 2003) and they analyse and process linguistic input (see Van Patten, 2004). Considering all these findings, language is more likely to be acquired with the kind of instruction which engages in psycholinguistics processing that occurs during SLA and also provides a focus on meaning. Although exposure to input is an important factor, it is also true that drawing learners' attention to the formal properties of an L2 language within a meaningful context (focus on form) might have a facilitative role and help learners to notice and process a particular form. As we said, this is one of the conditions that might help learners in acquiring an L2 more efficiently and speedily.

In order to explore whether there are particular approaches to focus on form better than others, we must first define what focus on form consists of, as this term has been used sometimes to express different meanings. Long (1991) and more recently Long and Robinson (1998) have distinguished two types of focus on form: 'focus on form' and 'focus on forms'. Doughty and Williams (1998) have defined 'focus on forms' as any type of instruction that isolates specific linguistic forms in order to teach them one at a time. Focus on forms refers to synthetic approaches to language teaching where the L2 is analysed in different parts such as grammar and vocabulary and these elements are taught in isolation from context. This type of approach to grammar teaching is found on structural syllabuses, where the syllabus consists of long and elaborate explanations of the grammatical rules of the target L2 followed by activities in which learners have to produce the target language through mechanical drills. This model of focus on forms has been criticized by scholars (Long and Robinson, 1998; Wong and Van Patten, 2003) particularly on the basis of the fact that L2 learners, rather than learning discrete lexical or grammatical items one at a time, follow predictable sequences in certain L2 features. As Doughty and Williams (1998:16) pointed out 'pedagogical materials and accompanying classroom procedures are designed to present and practise a series of linguistic items or forms'. In addition to this, L2 learners follow developmental sequences (Pienmann, 1998). L2 learners might have access to innate knowledge and analyse and process linguistic input. Therefore we should provide a similar condition to that present in L1 acquisition. (exposure to input, focus on communication, interaction and many opportunities to negotiate meaning).

Given that learners are not making measurable progress in their performance in this type of approach (structural syllabus), scholars and teachers turned their attention to a different kind of language syllabus, one that focuses on meaning (see following chapter). The underlying assumption was that L2 learners as L1 learners will have access to innate knowledge (Chomsky, 1965) and will need modified input for their interlanguage development. In the CLT approach (see following chapter) classroom practice should focus on meaning and input should be comprehensible to facilitate SLA. The main emphasis is on communication and expression of meaning rather than form. Krahsen Monitor theory (1982) is very much in line with this view claiming that exposure to comprehensible input is sufficient for L2 learners.

However, other scholars have sustained that some grammatical features (e.g. adverb placement and direct object in English by French learners, White, 1987) cannot be acquired with exposure to input alone. Lightbown and Spada (1990) have argued that learners can certainly acquire very high levels of fluency on an L2 through exposure to the input, as in the case of immersion courses; however, the level of accuracy they reach remains quite low.

Question to reflect on . . .

Can you think of an example of focus on form and focus on forms tasks/activities in Japanese?

Long (1991) first introduced the term 'focus on form' by suggesting that teaching should be meaning-focused but with some degree of attention to the grammatical properties of the language. Doughty and Williams (1998) defines a 'focus on form' as any type of instruction that encourages focus on meaning and a focus on form at the same time. This is to say that learners' attention is being focused on specific linguistic properties in the course of a communicative activity. The distinction, first used by Long, has been redefined by Spada (1997). Spada (1997:73) has defined, more generally, focus on form as 'any pedagogical effort which is used to draw the learners' attention to language form'. This can include an instructional intervention that seeks to attract learners' attention to formal features of an L2 within a meaningful context or a reaction to errors (corrective feedback). In many cases, a focus on form has been incorporated in a primarily communicative approach to language teaching. In Spada's view, grammar teaching should incorporate activities that focus on both meaning and form at the same time. Spada has argued (1997:77; see also Lightbown and Spada, 1999) that focus on form is generally more beneficial when L2 learners' attention is drawn to linguistic features in a less explicit way within a communicative teaching context. As pointed out by Takashima and Sugiura (2006) many teachers of Japanese have now begun to use communicative tasks in the language classroom. The use of tasks in the language classroom has attracted much attention (Nunan, 2001; Bygate, Skehan and Swain, 2001; Ellis, R. 2003) in language teaching as a tool to engage learners in real world situation. Tasks can be a useful instrument (see Part B of this book) to provide focus on form practice and draw learners' attention to particular linguistics features of an L2 while they are engaging in meaningful communication.

Focus on form can be accomplished in many ways; however, before we examine how we should provide for a focus on form we would like to deal with the following questions:

(1) Can learners focus on form and meaning simultaneously? (Terrell, 1986, 1991)
(2) What type of focus on form is available?

(1) Van Patten (1990) has investigated the effects of simultaneous attention to form and meaning in L2 learners. Van Patten measured the ability for low, intermediate and high proficiency university level learners to attend simultaneously to form and meaning. His findings suggest that learners find it difficult to attend to both form and meaning in the input they are exposed to. Van Patten (1990:296) has suggested that 'conscious attention to form in the input competes with conscious attention to meaning, and, by extension, that only when input is easily understood can learners attend to form as part of the intake process.' As a number of scholars have pointed out (Van Patten and Cadierno, 1993; Hulstijn 1989) L2 learners must attend to linguistic features in the input as well as to messages. However, excessive demands should not be put on learner's attentional resources. Van Patten (1996) claims that only when learners are familiar with the major lexical items in the input are they able to process the grammatical markers. He argues that when teachers focus on the grammatical properties of a target L2, they should make sure that learners are familiar with the lexical elements. Terrell (1991:60) concluded that 'instruction with little lexical load coupled with a high frequency of a single form–meaning relationship would result in helping learners to pay more attention and process non-salient, redundant grammatical forms'.

(2) In terms of what type of focus on form is available for teaching, two types of focus on form have been identified : proactive approaches and reactive approaches. Doughty and Williams (1998:198) have defined these two positions in this way: 'a proactive approach would entail selecting in advance an aspect of the target to focus on; whereas, a reactive stance would require that the teachers notice and be prepared to handle various learning difficulties as they arise.' Teachers might develop techniques to draw learners' attention to form during a communicative task or preselect a problematic linguistic feature to do so. As we said in the previous chapter, teachers must keep in mind some fundamentals concepts: they must consider developmental sequences, they must provide a refined input, they must take into consideration the complexity of the form/structure, they must take into consideration the L1 influence on SLA processes, they must focus primary on meaning. Some scholars have

developed proactive approaches to focus on form such as processing instruction (Van Patten, 1996, 2004) and input enhancement (Wong, 2005). These studies have shown that learners were able to notice and process linguistics features and include those linguistics features in their output. Ellis (1997, 2003) has advocated a more reactive focus on form which is more incidental, problem-oriented and output-based. Many empirical studies have been measured as a more reactive approach to focus on form such as corrective feedback and recast (Carroll and Swain, 1993; Doughty and Verela, 1998; Lyster and Ranta, 1997; Nobuyoshi and Ellis, 1993; Iwashita, 1999).

What type of focus on form?

As previously said, Doughty and Williams (1998) have made a distinction between reactive and proactive approaches to focus on form. In a proactive approach a grammar task (e.g. consciousness raising, processing instruction) is designed to ensure that there are opportunities to focus, process and use problematic forms while understanding or communicating a message. A reactive approach instead involves the use of a technique (e.g. recast) for drawing learner's attention to errors. SLA teachers and researchers have developed a series of instructional interventions to direct learners' attention to particular forms or structures of an L2 and therefore we present in this paragraph some proactive approaches to focus on form.

The most implicit type of focus on form is called 'input flood'. In this technique learners are simply exposed to the input that contains numerous instances of the same linguistics feature. By exposing learners to input flood, it is hoped that learners will notice a particular form of the target language. Flooding the input (without highlighting) with many examples of the same form will increase the frequency of the targeted form and hopefully L2 learners will have more chances to notice that form. As Gass (1997) pointed out, in order for the input to be usable for SLA, learners must attend to it or notice it in some ways. Input flood can be both written and oral. As suggested by Wong (2005), the idea is to expose learners over a period of time to many examples of the target item (increasing the frequency of the targeted form) via meaning-bearing input and comprehensible input (otherwise if learners struggle to extract meaning they will not notice the form).

Few studies have been conducted to measure the effectiveness of this approach (see studies conducted by Trahey and White, 1993 and Williams and Evans, 1998).

Question to reflect on . . .

Can you think of an example of how to flood the input with a Japanese linguistic feature?

A more explicit way to focus on form is the consciousness raising (CR) approach. It contrasts with traditional instruction (TI) in a number of ways. The most important of these differences is that in the CR approach greater attention is paid to the form–meaning relationship while there is an attempt to situate grammatical structure and element in questions within a broader discourse context. CR is an attempt to equip the learner with an understanding of a specific grammatical feature, developing a declarative rather than procedural knowledge of it (see Rutherford, 1987; Rutherford and Sharwood-Smith, 1988). The main characteristics of CR activities are (see Ellis, 1997:160–162; see also Ellis, 1991)

(1) isolating a particular linguistic feature;
(2) providing learners with some data which is an illustration of the target feature;
(3) asking learners to understand the feature; using further data to describe and explain in case of learner misunderstanding;
(4) asking learners to articulate the rule in the attempt to explain the grammatical structure.

Rutherford (1987) coined the term to refer to deliberate intervention to raise awareness in L2 learners about formal properties of a target language. The goal of consciousness raising is to make learners conscious of the rules that govern the use of particular language forms while providing the opportunity to engage in meaningful interaction. During CR tasks learners develop explicit knowledge about how the target language works and are pushed to negotiate meaning. Explicit knowledge should help learners notice that form in subsequent communicative input, while negotiation of meaning (interaction) can expose learners to more comprehensible input. During consciousness raising activities, learners are encouraged to discover the rules in consciousness raising. They are provided with some data and then asked to arrive (through some tasks) at an explicit understanding of some linguistic property of the target language. Raising consciousness about a particular form enable learners to notice it in communicative input. There is a clear distinction between traditional grammar instruction and CR as noted by Ellis (1997:160) as traditional practice is production-based whereas the main aim of CR is 'to construct a conscious representation of the target feature and to this end any production of the feature will be strictly limited and incidental'.

Few studies have been conducted tomeasure the effectiveness of this approach (see studies conducted by Fotos, 1993 and Fotos and Ellis, 1991).

Van Patten's view of grammar instruction, which will be examined in the next section, represents a step forward compared to Sharwood-Smith's position (1993) according to which, a way to provide formal instruction is to make some forms more salient in the input so that they come to learners attention. Processing instruction does not aim at raising learners' consciousness about grammatical form. As stated by Van Patten (1996:84) 'simply bringing a form to someone's attention is not a guarantee that it gets processed, for acquisition to happen the intake must continually provide the developing system with examples of correct form–meaning connections that are the results of input processing.' The ultimate scope of Van Patten's model (processing instruction) is not about raising consciousness awareness about a grammatical form but making the learner appreciate the communicative function of a particular form and consequently enrich the learner's intake

In the following section we will review some of the studies that have been carried out in order to ascertain whether there are particular types of focus on form which are more beneficial than others particularly in relation to the acquisition of Japanese. Some practical guidelines will be provided to develop focus on form grammatical tasks for the teaching of Japanese (practical examples of how to incorporate focus on form in a CLT approach will be presented and discussed in Chapter 4 of this book). Despite the fact that research on the use of different focus on form approaches has focused principally on English and romance languages, we will also examine some research data on the acquisition of Japanese as L2. Despite the limits in the database concerning classroom studies involving the acquisition of Japanese, two main lines of research have been identified:

studies on different types of input enhancement;
studies on the effects of processing instruction and structured input activities.

Input enhancement

Input enhancement has been defined by Sharwood-Smith (1991) as a process by which linguistic data will become more salient for L2 learners. This form of intervention (enhancing the input to allow learners to notice some specific forms in the input) should effect changes in learners' linguistic competence. Sharwood-Smith (1991, 1993) has proposed various techniques to enhance the input which varies in terms of explicitness and elaboration. A practical example would be to underline or to capitalize a specific grammatical item in a text to help learners notice that particular grammatical feature (textual enhancement, see sample material in Chapter 4).

A different technique would be to enhance typographically linguistic features (input flood). A practical example of this technique is to modify a text so that a particular target item would appear over and over again so that the text will contain many more exemplars of the same feature (see sample material in Chapter 4).

As Wong (2005:33) defined, explicitness refers to the sophistication and detail of the attention drawing (different degrees of information are provided, from metalinguistic information to seeing the target form highlighted), whereas elaboration refers to the depth and amount of time that is involved in implementing the enhancement technique (i.e. facial gesture, quizzical look). As highlighted by Wong (2005) input enhancement is a type of focus on form as opposed to focus on forms were learners' attention is drawn to isolated forms with no regard for meaning. As mentioned earlier, in order to help learners notice a particular feature we might want to provide learners with typographical cues such as bolding and italics to draw their attention to grammatical forms in the text. This technique is called textual enhancement and it is used to make particular features of written input more salient with the scope to help learners notice these forms and make form–meaning connections for. The target form is enhanced by visually altering its appearance in the text (italicized, bolded, underlined). Oral input enhancement can also be provided by using special stress, intonation and gestures in spoken input.

Question to reflect on . . .

Can you think of an example of a textual enhancement activity in Japanese?

In the following chapter we will provide examples of how we can use these techniques to enhance the input in the teaching of Japanese.

Studies on different types of input enhancement

Considering the fact that a great deal of SLA takes place through exposure to language in the input, the effects of less explicit approaches to grammar instruction have been investigated (see Doughty, 1991). Classroom studies on the effects of input enhancement in the acquisition of Japanese as an L2 are limited and have several methodological problems. Moroishi (1999) conducted a study where explicit and implicit learning conditions were compared. Learners of Japanese were assigned to three groups (explicit, implicit and control) and received instruction on the acquisition of four types of Japanese conjectural auxiliaries: -*yoo da*, -*soo da*, -*rashii* and -*daroo*. The explicit group received grammar explanation which was followed by meaning-focused reading activities. The implicit group received no grammar explanation and they engaged in the same reading activities. However, the target forms were enhanced in the text (underlined). The main findings from this study showed that both groups improved after receiving the instructional treatment, but it was the explicit group that performed better. Kubota (1999) provided similar evidence in a study comparing grammar instruction vs. input enhancement on the acquisition of gerund forms of Japanese true adjectives (*i*-adjectives) and nominal adjectives (*na*-adjectives). The explicit group outperformed the implicit group. As pointed out by Moroishi (2003:143) the results of these studies have some methodological problems: 'measurements employed in these studies generally favoured explicit treatments. Implicit treatments might require longer post-intervention observation periods for learning to be detected.'

Therefore we might conclude that the overall results of this line of classroom research (further studies in Japanese should be conducted to address some of the limitations and problems previously outlined) seem to indicate that a type of focus on form which is implemented through different enhancement techniques (drawing learners' attention in meaningful ways to the use of target structures in context) may facilitate acquisition. However, as argued by Van Patten (1996) and Wong (2005) the fact that learners pay attention to enhanced forms, is not a guarantee that those forms will be automatically internalized by the learners.

Processing instruction

Input processing and processing instruction

Cadierno, (1995:180) has pointed out that research in SLA has been mainly concerned with whether or not instruction has an effect on different aspects of language acquisition neglecting the fundamental questions of why and how instruction would make a difference in SLA. Therefore, one possible way of researching the causes of the effects of instruction on SLA is to look at the interaction between instruction to which learners are exposed and the way learners process input.

Terrell (1991:56) has examined the role of grammar instruction and has posited one crucial question 'what psycholinguistic processes are utilized in input processing?'

As suggested by Van Patten (1996), the learners work on an internal schedule when it comes to grammatical developments. Therefore to investigate the role of instruction in SLA we should seek to explain the psycholinguistic processes utilized in input processing.

One of the main implications for instruction drawn from previous sections is that instruction should take into account the psycholinguistic processes utilized in input processing (strategies and mechanisms used by L2 learners to process input). The main role for instruction in the processing instruction (PI) framework is to manipulate, enhance and alter input processing in order to make intake grammatically richer. PI takes, as its point of departure, what we know about how grammatical forms and structures are acquired.

Research on input processing theory (see Van Patten 1990, 1996) has focused on issues such as how learners process input, what part of the input becomes intake, an insight into the processes involved and strategies used by learners to decode and store linguistic information and the role of attention required. Van Patten (1996:17) has suggested that the central issue for SLA is 'how learners' internal processors allocate attentional resources during online processing'. Therefore, the question to be asked is 'what causes certain stimuli in the input to be detected and not others?' The input processing capacity of L2 learners is limited as only certain features will receive attention at any given time during the processing of a sentence. Van Patten (1996, 2002, 2004) has identified some processing principles used by learners to decode input. He has indicated two main principles and each principle is composed of sub-principles (see Figure 2.1). The two principles are:

Principle 1 (P1). The Primacy of Meaning Principle: Learners process input for meaning before they process for form.

Principle 2 (P2). The First Noun Principle: Learners tend to process the first noun or pronoun they encounter in a sentence as the subject or agent.

PRINCIPLE 1

Principle 1. Learners' process input for meaning before they process it for form.

P 1a. The Primacy of Content Words Principle: learners process content words in the input before anything else.

P 1b. The Lexical Preference Principle: learners will tend to rely on lexical items as opposed to grammatical form to get meaning when both encode the same semantic information.

P 1c. The Preference for Nonredundancy Principle: learners are more likely to process nonredundant meaningful grammatical form before they process redundant meaningful forms.

P 1d. The Meaning-Before-Nonmeaning Principle: learners are more likely to process meaningful grammatical forms before nonmeaningful forms irrespective of redundancy.

P 1e. The Availability of Resources Principle: for learners to process either redundant meaningful grammatical forms or nonmeaningful forms, the processing of overall sentential meaning must not drain available processing resources.

P 1f. The Sentence Location Principle: learners tend to process items in the initial position of the sentence before those in final position and in medial position.

PRINCIPLE 2

Principle 2. The First Noun Principle: Learners tend to process the first noun or pronoun they encounter in a sentence as the subject or agent.

P 2a. The Lexical Semantics Principle: learners may rely on lexical semantics, where possible, instead of word order to interpret sentences.

P 2b. The Event Probabilities Principle: learners may rely on event probabilities, where possible, instead of word order to interpret sentences.

P 2c. The Contextual Constraint Principle: learners may rely less on the First Noun Principle if preceding context constraints the possible interpretation of a clause or sentence.

Figure 2.1 (Adapted form Van Patten, 2004:15).

The main concern in input processing is how learners initially perceive and process linguistic data in the language they hear and how they make form–meaning connections. PI will help learners make form–meaning connections (connecting particular meanings to particular forms (grammatical or lexical).

The first sub-principle (P1a) stated that learners will focus on content words during comprehension. In the following sentence in Japanese *Kinō watashi wa gakko ni itta* (Yesterday, I went to school), learners will struggle to process verb forms and will process content words first.

In the second sub-principle (P1.b) of the first principle, the so-called Lexical Preference Principle, Van Patten claims (1996) that learners prefer processing lexical items to grammatical items (e.g. morphology) for semantic information. This principle is a direct consequence of the first sub-principle (P1a) proposed by Van Patten. A great number of grammatical features encode some kind of semantic information. In the case of verbal inflection in Japanese the verbal inflection -*mashita* encodes past as in *ikimashita*. However, this semantic notion is also expressed in Japanese by words such as *Kinō* (yesterday) or *Kyonen* (last year). Given that, as postulated in the first Principle (P1), learners are driven to process content words before anything else, they would attend to temporal reference of 'pastness' before verbal inflection of the past tense. Learners will mark time early in the acquisition of verb morphology through lexical items and only subsequently add verb tense markings. In the following sentence in Japanese *Kinō watashi wa gakko ni itta* (Yesterday I went to school) learners will process the lexical item (*Kinō*) before the grammatical item (*itta*). The acquisition of past tense in Japanese is affected by the Lexical Preference Principle. In a sentence (see below) containing a lexical item such as Kino (yesterday)

Kinō	watashi wa	gakko ni	itta
Yesterday	I	to school	went

the grammatical form *itta* (went) tends not to be processed as learners will process the lexical item for pastness first. This will cause a delay in the acquisition of past tense morphology.

In the third sub-principle (P1c), Van Patten (1996:24) suggests that 'it is the relative communicative value of a grammatical form that plays a major role in determining the learner's attention to it during input processing and the likelihood of its becoming detected and thus part of intake.' Van Patten has stated that L2 learners prefer processing more meaningful morphology rather than less or nonmeaningful morphology. Communicative value refers to the contribution made to the meaning of an utterance by a linguistic form. In order to establish whether a linguistic form has low or high communicative value, we need to follow two criteria:

(1) Inherent referential meaning
(2) Semantic redundancy

In the following Japanese sentence *Kinō Kyoto ni ikimashita* (Yesterday, I went to *Kyoto*) the past tense is a redundant past marker. Furthermore, since *Kino* has marked the sentence as past, the past markers on subsequent verbs are also redundant.

The sixth sub-principle (P1f) lays out a specific hierarchy of difficulty with regard to L2 features. In a sentence like *Kinō kaisha ni ikimashita* (Yesterday, I went to the office) the easiest forms to process are those located in initial position (*Kinō*) within an utterance. A more difficult form to process occurs in utterance-final position (*ikimashita*).

In the second principle (P2), Van Patten (1996) argues that learners tend to process the first noun or pronoun they encounter in a sentence as the subject or agent. In Japanese word order, an object is often placed before the subject (OSV) and the verb at the end of the sentence. The First Noun Principle might affect language processing. In the sentence Chris hit Maria (see below), learners might process Maria as the subject of the sentence and this will lead to a misinterpretation of the sentence and delay in acquisition.

Maria o	Chris wa	nagutta
Maria	Chris	hit

Japanese allows L2 learners to express the same content by more than one word order like SOV, OSV, OV. Apart from the word order example provided, other linguistic features are affected by the First Noun principle in Japanese (see Hikima, forthcoming):

a. case marker
b. comparative
c. passive

(a) Kumakun wa Yoshikocahn o sukidesu (SOV)
   Yoshikocahn o Kumakun wa sukidesu (OSV)
   Both sentences are possible and mean 'Kuma likes Yoshiko.'
(b) watashi no hooga anata yori utsukushii (I am more beautiful than you.)
   anata yori watashi no hooga utsukushii (I am more beautiful than you.)
(c) neko wa   inu ni   oikakerareta (A cat was chased by a dog)
       cat   dog   was chased

This sentence must be interpreted by L2 learners as if it was the cat that chased the dog as L2 learners would process the first item in the sentence as the agent (subject) of the sentence.

We now have some idea of what learners are doing with input when they are asked to comprehend it and therefore we can begin to develop a new kind of grammar instruction that will guide and focus learners' attention to grammatical elements of a sentence when they process input. The main aim of PI is 'to push to get L2 learners to make form–meaning mappings in order to create grammatically richer intake' (Van Patten 1996:55) through structure input activities. The two main characteristics (see chapter four for a full examination, discussion and sample activities) of PI are:

(a) Explicit information regarding forms and processing strategies;
(b) Structured input practice.

Question to reflect on . . .

Can you think of other linguistic features (forms or structures) in Japanese affected by input processing principles?

Studies on the effects of the different components of processing instruction

One important line of PI research is the one that has isolated the three components of PI (explicit information, information about psycholinguistic processes, structured input practice) with the intention of establishing which factor is responsible for the positive results obtained in the studies we have previously reviewed. Van Patten and Oikkenon (1996) carried out the first study to investigate whether the results obtained in Van Patten and Cadierno (1993) were due to the explicit information components or to the positive effects of the other component of PI, namely the structured input activities.

Participants in this study were all studying Spanish at intermediate level. The item investigated was the same as in Van Patten and Cadierno's study (1993): object pronouns in Spanish. The materials, design, assessment tasks were also the same as the main purpose of the research was to establish which of the following variables, explanation, structured input activities or combination of the two, is the most significant in accounting for the post-tests results. Three groups tested followed the same design as Van Patten and Cadierno (1993), one receiving only explicit instruction; the other structured input activities and the third full PI. The outcome of this study was that structured input activities were found responsible for learners' gains. The gains made (on both the interpretation and production tasks) by both the PI and the structured input activities group were greater than the group receiving only explicit instruction on the targeted form. A very significant finding of this study is that the structured input activities group performed as well as the PI group. As indicated by Van Patten (1996:126), these findings strongly suggest that it is the structured input activities itself and the form–meaning connections being made during input processing that are responsible for the relative effects observed in the present and previous studies.

Benati (2004a) reports an experimental investigation of the relative effects of PI, structured input activities and explicit information on the acquisition of future tense. The study addressed the Lexical Preference Principle (P1b.). The material and assessment measures were the same as the ones used for the study carried out comparing PI vs. TI (Benati, 2001). The population was divided into three groups receiving respectively: PI, structured input only, explicit information only. The results confirmed the findings obtained in the Van Patten and Oikkenon's study (1996). A further replication study was conducted by Benati (2004a, 2004b) on the acquisition of Italian of gender agreement and future tense. This study addressed the Preference for Nonredundancy Principle (P1c.). The structured input activities were developed with the intention of helping learners to process the target form efficiently and correctly. English native speakers studying Italian at undergraduate level were the population in this study. Even in this case, subjects were divided into three groups: the first received PI, the second group structured input only, the third group explicit information only. One interpretation and two production measures were used in a pre- and post-test design. Once more the results were similar to those of Van Patten and Oikkenon, 1996. The PI group and the structured input group made significant gains on a sentence-level interpretation test and sentence-level production tests, while the explicit information group made no gains. The structured input group also made identical gains to the PI group in the oral production task, compared to the explicit information group.

Farley (2004b) conducted a study measuring the effects of PI and structured input activities only on the acquisition of Spanish subjunctive of doubt (Sentence Location Principle (P1f.) was the relevant processing principle). In this study Farley used the same materials, assessment tasks and analyses as those used by Farley (2004a). Two groups participated. One received full PI and the other SI practice. The results were slightly different than the previous ones.

Despite the fact that both groups made significant improvements from pre- to post-tests, the PI group outperformed the SI practice group both in the interpretation and the production task.

Wong (2004b) found positive results for SI practice alone in a study where she compared the effects of PI, SI practice, EI only and a control group in the acquisition of French negative + indefinite article. In a negative or nonaffirmative statement (*ne . . . pas*), *de* is used before nouns beginning with consonant or *d'* before nouns beginning with vowel. However, learners, due to the Lexical Preference Principle (P1b.) will first process *ne . . . pas* before *de* or *d'* to get the meaning of the French negation. Intermediate students of French participated in this study. The materials were designed to alter the processing problem, and an interpretation and a production task were developed. The results in both the interpretation and the production task showed that both the PI group and the SI group were not different and better than the EI group and the control group. The SI component seemed to be the causative factor for the beneficial effects of PI.

Lee and Benati (2007a) extended previous research which suggested that learners' strategy for processing input could be altered through structured input activities which eventually enhance the acquisition of the target grammar feature, by comparing the relative effects of two types of instructional interventions (SIA vs. TI) on the acquisition of Japanese past tense form. This feature of Japanese was selected because of the processing principles investigated in this study: The 'Lexical Preference Principle'. In a sentence such as *Kinō kaisha ni ikimashita* (Yesterday, I went to the office) both the lexical item *Kinō* and the verb ending *ikimashita* communicate past tense.

Again the main purpose of SIA in this study is to push learners to process the past tense marker that otherwise may not be processed as learners do not need to process it to assign 'pastness' to the meaning of the sentence. All subjects were Italian native speakers and were studying Japanese in a school. Subjects were assigned to two groups. Two sets of materials were developed. One for the TI group which consisted in grammar teaching and output practice and one for the SIA group which involved teaching the subjects to process input sentences. The output-based activities required the subjects to produce accurately past tense forms. The SIA required learners to interpret sentences containing past tense forms and make form–meaning connections.

Two tests were produced: one for the interpretation task and one for the production task. The results of the interpretation and the production data confirmed the key role for structured input activities practice. The evidence collected in this study has shown that SIA is a better instructional treatment than TI practice as the SIA group outperformed the TI group in the interpretation task and the two instructional groups improved equally in the production task.

Another study which has involved the acquisition of Japanese, is the study conducted by Lee and Benati (2007b). In their previous research (2007a) on processing the Japanese past tense and the present tense forms, they found that structured input activities enhanced learners' processing of the form. Learners who received SIA made significant gains on both interpretation and production tests. The question that Lee and Benati (2007b) addressed in this new study for both past and present tense in Japanese was whether learners who receive SIA with input enhancements make greater gains than those who only receive SIA. Two groups were used, one receiving SIA enhanced and the other SIA unenhanced.

The instructional material was the same SIA activities; however, learners receiving the enhanced version were exposed to enhanced aural and written stimuli. In aural activities, the targeted verb ending was enhanced by raising the teacher's voice (louder) and by tightening the muscles of the phonal apparatus (tenser). In written activities, the targeted endings were bolded and underlined (not the entire verb) so that attention to the verbal element was drawn. The two linguistic forms were the present tense and past tense forms; the two main processing principles were the Lexical Preference and the Sentence Location. Japanese past tense morphology is an inflection that appears in word final position (-*mashita*). Japanese present tense morphology is also an inflection that also appears in word final position. The morphology for affirmed verbs (-*masu*) is different from those for negated verbs (-*masen*). Standard Japanese word order places the verb (and its markings) in sentence final position. The past tense marker is high in communicative value when it is the only indicator of tense. The marker's communicative value drops when it co-occurs with a lexical temporal indicator. The lexical temporal indicator makes the verb morphology redundant. Additionally, standard Japanese word order places the lexical temporal indicator in the initial position of the sentence. It would be the first sentence element learners encounter whereas the verb morphology would be the last. The semantic distinction between affirmative and negative verbal propositions is conveyed through word final, sentence final morphology. Learners will have to attend to the morphological difference between *shimasu* and *shimasen* to determine whether a proposition (studying) is affirmed or negated.

The findings from this study showed that both enhanced and unenhanced group made similar gains from pre to post-tests in both the interpretation and the production tasks. This confirms that it is the nature of structured input practice that is responsible for learners' improved performance and not whether a form is enhanced or unenhanced.

The main finding of the second line of research in PI confirmed that it is the structured input component practice that is responsible for the changes in learners developing system and eventually in their output. As a result of the empirical evidence collected in the research which has compared PI vs. its components; we are able to conclude that the causative factor in the positive effects for PI is due to the effects of the structured input activities. These have been proved and observed in different processing principles, languages, linguistic items and assessment tasks. Structured input activities, within PI, represent the most significant variable. As indicated by Van Patten (1996:126), structured input activities and the form–meaning connections being made during input processing are responsible for the relative effects observed.

Box 2.1 Arguments in favour of grammar teaching: summary

Drawing from what we said in the previous chapter and this chapter we might conclude the following about the role of focus on form:

1) Noticing and awareness play an important role in L2 learning (noticing hypothesis).
2) Given the fact that L2 learners go through developmental stages, grammar teaching can be beneficial for certain structures taught at the right time (readiness).
3) Considering the existence of processing constraints, grammar instruction should aim at restructuring the input so that learners can make right form–meaning connections.

Summary

Although input is the main and essential ingredient for acquisition with learners engaged in activities that are meaning focused so that they can process input, grammar instruction has an important role to play (see Box 2.1). As argued by Wong and Van Patten (2003) paradigmatic explanation of the rules of an L2 and drill practice are not effective ways to focus on form in the language classroom. However, certain types of approaches to grammar instruction could be a useful tool to make certain forms in the input more salient so that learners would notice them and perhaps process them more quickly. Enhancing the salience of features in the input does not automatically mean that enhanced input will become intake. We cannot control whether or not learners process input correctly and efficiently. Sharwood-Smith (1993) cautioned that we can increase the chance that learners will attend to a target form. We provide learners with supplementary doses of comprehensible input and boost the likelihood that they will notice what they need to in order to enhance the process of SLA. However as argued by Wong (2005), we cannot expect learners to be able to use the target forms immediately in production, as form–meaning connections need to be strengthened before they can be accessed for accurate production. While a focus on form incorporated in a communicative framework of language teaching is desirable, explicit information is not a pedagogical technique that relies on the provision of input (see results of PI components studies). Learners need to have access to a great amount of comprehensible and meaning-bearing input, and explicit information does not necessarily provide learners with additional amount of input. Furthermore, it takes time away from providing students with input and meaningful language use. The challenge, as suggested by Lee and Van Patten (1995, 2003) is how to incorporate grammar teaching in the language classroom so that learners are still mainly involved in communicative activities.

In Chapter 1, we have noted that research in instructed SLA has revealed the limited role of instruction. However, this does not mean that in a communicative approach to language teaching we should renounce the teaching of grammar. Instructors should provide comprehensible input in the language classroom. Comprehensible input should be directed to the learners' acquisition of grammar, vocabulary and other linguistic features. In this chapter, we have presented two different approaches to grammar teaching and one approach to corrective feedback in line with current theories of language learning. Although, there has been very little focus on investigating the effects of focus on form in the acquisition of Japanese, the main findings of studies which have been reviewed in this chapter can be summarized as follows:

(1) Studies measuring the role of formal instruction and particularly the effects of different types of focus on form seem to support the view that encouraging learners to pay attention to the formal properties of language in a communicative context may facilitate acquisition (Spada, 1987). A type of

form which is provided in the context of communicative instruction, should aim at alternating a focus on meaning and a focus on form. The overall results of these studies (see Doughty and Williams, 1998 for a review) seem to show that in those cases where a focus on form component has been included in a CLT programme there have been positive benefits in terms of learners' knowledge and performance. The question is not whether or not we can incorporate a focus on form, but how we can do so;

(2) Despite the fact that studies on the effects of approaches such as input flood and input enhancement, reviewed in this chapter, seem to provide mixed results, we can argue that they are alternative and implicit ways to provide a focus on form. They are an effective way to integrate grammar instruction with the provision of opportunities for meaning-focused use of the target language. If learners notice certain salient forms (Schmidt, 1990) because of frequency they are more likely to acquire them than they are to acquire forms they have not noticed. However, even if a learner has noticed a form without a communication need, acquisition might be delayed. It is therefore vital to help learners making form–meaning connections and to tell them what to pay attention to, what to notice and why they must change their processing particular items in the sentence.

PI is a type of grammar instruction which is superior to output-based instruction and has an effect on the way in which learners' process input. These effects are observable in the learner output. SIA practice is an effective form of intervention in altering processing principles and providing a focus on forms that help L2learners to make correct and efficient form–meaning mappings.

There have been considerable changes in terms of second language instruction and there is a particular need for a change in the way Japanese is taught. In recent years, we have witnessed a change in the way Japanese is taught in the foreign language classroom. Teachers are not relying on structural syllabi any longer and teachers use a wide range of communicative and interaction tasks. They have moved away from the use of mechanical and audio-lingual drills. Much of this has been undoubtedly the shift from the explicit focus on language itself (i.e. grammar, phonology and vocabulary) to an emphasis (implicit focus) on the expression and comprehension of meaning through language. Behind this shift is the belief that learners can develop greater second language communicative abilities through the kind of instruction that focus on both form and meaning.

The question is not whether or not we should include a focus on form component in the teaching of Japanese grammar; the question is how to best incorporate a focus on form component (instructional techniques and corrective feedback) in Japanese language teaching methodology. The main implications for grammar teaching in classroom studies investigating the role of focus on form are as follows:

- given that acquisition can be more effectively influenced by manipulating input rather than output, grammar tasks should be developed to ensure that learners process input correctly and efficiently;
- grammar tasks should be designed for learners to notice and process forms in the input and make correct form-mapping connections;
- language teaching should include a variety of grammar tasks that invite both a focus on form and a focus on meaning (see Box 2.2).

In Chapter 4, we will provide guidelines to develop such a tasks in the teaching of Japanese.

Box 2.2   Grammar teaching proactive approaches

1) Consciousness raising
2) Input Enhancement techniques
3) Processing Instruction

More questions to reflect on . . .

(1) What is the role of grammar instruction in Japanese L2 teaching? Is grammar taught in a traditional way?
(2) Can you find more classroom studies in the acquisition of Japanese which have investigated the effects of different types of focus on form approaches?
(3) What are the key concepts and key evidence of the different approaches for grammar teaching reviewed in this chapter?
(4) Can you read the following study in Japanese (The effects of structured input activities on the acquisition of two linguistics features. In Lee, J. F. and Benati, A. G. (2007a) *Delivering Processing Instruction in Classrooms and Virtual Contexts: Theory and Practice (49–69).* London: Equinox) and highlight the main findings?

Key terms

Consciousness raising: this term refers to a particular approach to grammar teaching which intends to raise consciousness on a specific grammatical form/structure in a targeted L2.

Focus on form: we define focus on form as any proactive or reactive attempt to provide learners with a focus on some linguistics properties of a target language. Focus on form is different than focus on forms.

Input enhancement techniques: this term refers to a particular approach to focus on form which attempts to bring a particular form/structure to L2 learners' focal attention by enhancing the input through the use of different techniques.

Processing instruction: this term refers to a type of focus on form whose main aim is to alter L2 learners' strategies by restructuring the input. The main aim of processing instruction is helping learners to process grammatical forms/structures in the input.

Further reading

Benati, A. and Lee, J. F. (2008). *Secondary and Cumulative effects.* Clevedon: Multilingual Matters.

Benati, A. and Lee, J. F. (2009). *Processing Instruction and Discourse.* London: Continuum.

Doughty, C. and Williams, J. (Eds) (1998). *Focus on Form in Classroom Second language Acquisition.* Cambridge: CUP.

Ellis, R. (1997). *SLA Research and Language Teaching.* Oxford: OUP.

Farley, A. (2005). *Structured Input: Grammar Instruction for the Acquisition-Oriented Classroom.* New York: McGraw-Hill.

Lee, J. F. and Benati, A. G. (2007a). *Delivering Processing Instruction in Classrooms and Virtual Contexts: Theory and Practice.* London: Equinox.

Lee, J. F. and Benati, A. G. (2007b). *Second Language Processing: An Analysis of Theories, Problems and Possible Solutions.* London: Continuum.

Otha, A. S. (2001a). *Second Language Acquisition Process in the Classroom: Learning Japanese.* Mahwah, NJ: Lawrence Erlbaum Associates.

Wong, W. (2005). *Input Enhancement: From Theory and Research to the Classroom.* New York: McGraw-Hill.

Part B
Communicative Language Teaching: Grammar and Communicative Tasks

In Part B of this book, we present and examine Communicative Language Teaching. Practical suggestions aimed at developing communicative tasks in the teaching of Japanese will be proposed. In Chapter 3 we provide an overview of the CLT approach.

In Chapter 4, three main approaches to grammar teaching (focus on form) will be reviewed and guidelines to develop grammar tasks to teach Japanese provided. In Chapter 5, we will discuss and present how various communicative tasks to teach Japanese can be developed.

Communicative Language Teaching 3

Introduction

At the theoretical level, major findings (see Chapters 1 and 2 in this book) in SLA research have challenged previous methodologies in language teaching and have prepared the path for a new and more communicative approach to the teaching of a second language. As previously said one of the first and more important findings in SLA research to emerge was that acquisition orders do not match instructional orders. Learners follow a particular path in the way to develop the L2 system regardless of the order in which grammatical features are taught. A second and also crucial finding is that explicit grammar instruction does not affect natural stages of development. Learners tend to pass through predicted stages (Pienemman, 1998). As pointed out by Lee and Van Patten (1995, 2003) communicative language ability develops as learners engage in communication and not as result of habit-formation grammatical items. On the basis of main findings in classroom research investigating the effects of different approaches to grammar instruction, it was argued in Chapter 2 that the acquisition of grammar is more a function of the learner than the instructor. Research findings on the effects of grammar instruction, have revealed that its effects are limited at best; however, a focus on form could be beneficial if it is incorporated in a communicative framework of language teaching (Spada, 1987). In addition to that, we have argued that one way in which grammar instruction seems to be successful is by altering the way L2 learners process input. These arguments were based on the assumption that the acquisition of grammar appears to be a result of some internal mechanism that processes, organizes and stores language data and that comprehensible and meaning bearing input seems to be the essential ingredient for this to happen (Krashen, 1982; Gass, 1997). At the practical and pedagogical level, the main question asked by many teachers is: why does a child learn his L1 with relative ease while a learner finds it very difficult to learn an L2 in the classroom? One of the possible reasons for this is that the classroom environment is often an artificial setting and language teaching and learning lacks authenticity. The challenging question is whether we can recreate authenticity in the classroom through our teaching. In the traditional classroom instructional environment, the focus is on the language itself. Learners must master the grammatical rules of the target language where the emphasis is on learning the language rather than using the language for communicative purposes. Communicative instruction should recreate the same conditions of a natural setting and place more emphasis on interaction, conversation and language use rather than on learning the language.

CLT has been influenced by Krashen input theory (1982). There are certain practical implications for classroom practice consistent with Krashen's theory (1982) which has been summarized by Terrel (1977):

- beginning language instruction should focus on communicative competence rather than on grammatical perfection;
- instruction has to aim at the modification and improvement of the student's developing grammar rather than at building up that grammar (see Chapter four in this book);
- create the opportunity for students to acquire rather than force them to learn language;
- affective rather than cognitive factors are primary in language learning;
- the key to comprehension and oral production is the acquisition of vocabulary;
- three types of activities should dominate the classroom lesson: comprehension activities, role plays and group problem solving tasks (see Chapter five in this book).

CLT is certainly a kind of instruction that has received a great deal of attention in recent years. In the 1980s, one could talk of a 'fever' for the

CLT approach. Johnson (1982) considers CLT to be a type of instruction which emerged from the growing discontent on the part of language teachers with previous methods of teaching, together with the need for a new method which would essentially bring the learner into closer contact with the target language community. Littlewood (1981) claimed that CLT makes us consider language not only in terms of its structures but also in terms of the communicative functions that it performs. Therefore, according to Littlewood this approach aims at understanding what people do with language forms when they communicate.

As previously mentioned, the way Japanese is taught in the foreign language classroom has changed. Teachers of Japanese do not rely on a structural syllabus any longer and Japanese is taught in a more communicative way. Learners are encouraged to practice the language for communication purposes and therefore classroom tasks have increasingly become more communicative.

The communicative approach to language teaching

Linguistics and socio-linguistics influences

The CLT approach is based on the assumption that it will lead to the development of both linguistic competence (knowledge of the rules of grammar) and communicative competence (a knowledge of the rules of language use). The development of a new communicative approach to language teaching is a complex one which is related to a number of disciplines. Chomsky's criticism (1965) of behaviourist learning theories, in undermining the credibility of ALM, sets the framework for a more child-centred approach which favours a highly inductive approach. Chomsky has argued (1965) that language acquisition cannot be the result of a process of habit formation through imitation and repetition. He argues that the exposure to linguistic data triggers the Language Acquisition Device which is the device responsible for acquisition. This device helps learners seek the rules governing language through exposure to comprehensible input. His view is that acquisition is an internal process and not an external one as in the case of behaviourism. Chomsky's view of competence is limited to linguistic competence as he believes that the linguistics competence that is innate in children, will lead to internalization of the rules of the language. Hymes (1972) reacts to this narrow view on the basis that it concentrates knowledge of the language only, taking no account of the social context in which it takes place. He proposes a broader notion of competence that he called communicative competence. Hymes views language as affected by a variety of social factors in specific contexts. He distinguishes between linguistic and sociolinguistics competence. Linguistic competence is the knowledge of grammatical rules (i.e. lexical items and rules of syntax and morphology). Sociolinguistics competence refers to knowledge of the rules of language performance.

Halliday (1973) claims that language is a form of interaction through which children can learn. Language has several functional roles and it is used as a communicative tool in social interactions. According to Halliday, learning a language is not just a matter of acquiring grammatical knowledge; learning a language is concerned with the ability to use the language. In his view, language is a form of interaction and learners acquire the language through using the language in interactive situations. This implies that learners should be encouraged to interact using language to communicate as grammatical knowledge is learned through using the language socially.

Communicative competence

Communicative competence (see Box 3.1) is the most important concept at the base of the advent of CLT. Canale and Swain (1980) argue that the communicative approach is to focus on grammatical forms, language functions, appropriateness, rules of discourse, registers and sociocultural contexts. Communicative competence comprises the knowledge of the grammatical system of an L2 as well as the knowledge of the social and cultural contexts. Learners of Japanese will need to learn the grammatical system of the language as well as having an understanding of how the language is used in different cultural and social contexts.

Communicative language competence is made up of various components (see Figure 3.1, adapted from Bacham and Palmer (1996). Although it appears that language ability is divided into hierarchical components of language knowledge, all these components interact with each other and with features of the language use situation. It is the interaction between knowledge and language use in context that characterizes communicative language use. Language competence involves two components: language knowledge and strategic competence. Language knowledge includes two broad categories: organizational knowledge and pragmatic knowledge. Organizational knowledge is concerned with how the utterances or sentences and texts are organized. It comprises the

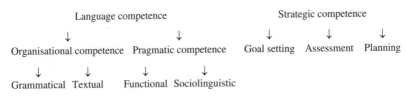

Figure 3.1 Communicative competence (Adapted from Bacham and Palmer (1996:66–73)).

abilities involved in controlling the formal structure of language for producing or recognizing grammatically correct sentences, understanding their content and ordering them to form texts. It is divided into grammatical knowledge (how individual utterances or sentences are organized) and textual knowledge (how utterances or sentences are organized to form texts). Grammatical knowledge includes knowledge of vocabulary, syntax, phonology and graphology. Textual knowledge (how utterances or sentences are organized to form texts) is divided into two areas: knowledge of cohesion (relationship between sentences in written texts: use of conjunction, lexical cohesion, reference) and knowledge of rhetorical (how texts or conversations are organized: narration, comparison, ordering information in paragraphs, introduction, conclusion; conversation: attention grabbing).

Pragmatic knowledge relates utterances or sentences and texts to their meaning, to the intentions of language users (what does she/he really want to say?), and to the general characteristics of the language use setting (is it appropriate to say this like that in this context?). It is divided into two areas: functional knowledge and sociolinguistic knowledge. Functional knowledge enables us to understand the relationship between utterances or sentences and texts and the intentions of language users.

Question to reflect on . . .

How do you measure communicative competence? Can you think of an assessment task in Japanese to measure grammatical, sociolinguistics, discourse or strategic competence?

Sociolinguistic knowledge enables us to create or interpret language that is appropriate to a particular language use setting: for example writing a letter to a friend or writing a letter to a company. This includes knowledge of the dialect, registers, natural or idiomatic expressions, and cultural references and figures of speech. Strategic competence would include the following:

Goal setting (deciding what I am going to do);
Assessment (what do I need to complete this task?, what do I have to wowith?);
Planning (how I am going to use what I know?).

The goal of CLT is for learners exposed to an L2 to achieve communicative competence.

Box 3.1   Communicative competence: summary

1) Grammatical competence: knowledge of the linguistic form or structure of a target language.
2) Discourse competence: knowledge of how sentences connect for discourse (cohesion and coherence).
3) Sociolinguistics competence: knowledge of use of the language in an appropriate way.
4) Strategic competence: knowledge of how to cope with the L2 target language when we do not possess a full knowledge of the language.

Wilkins and the functional-notional syllabus

Wilkins (1974, 1976) has proposed a new language syllabus based on the meanings which learners need to express when they use the target language. The syllabus is therefore constructed on the basis of notions and functions (functional syllabus). Notions refer to the meanings and concepts learners need in order to communicate in the target language (e.g. time, duration, location). Functions are the language learners need in order to accomplish different communicative tasks such as asking for something, presenting somebody, suggesting, inviting, describing, etc. In questioning the adequacy of the grammatical syllabus which consists of a sequence of graded grammatical items he recognizes the importance of constructing a syllabus that is communicatively organized. Wilkins's syllabus is an attempt to design a new syllabus that takes into account the communicative aspects of language (learners' needs, use of language in social contexts, language appropriateness, use of language for interaction and communication) without ignoring linguistics components.

Widdowson (1990:157) sustains that language learning is about competence and performance, and a structural syllabus only helps learners to develop a knowledge of the language (grammatical aspects of the language) to meet the requirements of conventional examinations. He argues (1990:158) the

> disadvantages of the structural approach is that it does not allow the learners to use language in a natural way. They tend to fixate on form for its own sake, internalize the language system as a separate body of knowledge and fail to learn for themselves how to use it.

Main characteristics

The main characteristic of CLT (see Box 3.2) is that it is a student-centred type of instruction, a very revolutionary approach to foreign language teaching as it concerns both teaching and learning. If the class can become 'an area of cooperative negotiation, joint interpretation, and the sharing of expression' as indicated by Breen and Candlin (1980), then the teacher is in the position to give the students the opportunity for spontaneous, unpredictable exploratory production of language when involved in classroom activities. If this is combined with the opportunity for making mistakes and teacher tolerance, the students can interact with their peers who have also had the message conveyed to them without being afraid of overcorrection. This is part of the aim of producing fluency and developing comprehension. The main contribution of this new type of instruction is the shift away from attention to the grammatical forms to the communicative properties of the language. The teacher creates the opportunity and the conditions in the classroom in a communicative way. This is to say that the student has 'someone to talk to, something to talk about, and a desire to understand and to make himself understood' (Mitchell, 1988). If that happens, the learning can take place naturally and teaching can be effective. This emphasis on the communicative properties of the language does not mean that accuracy must be sacrificed for the sake of fluency. However, it must not inhibit the natural use of language in the classroom context when the students interact (Brumfit, 1984).

At classroom level CLT possesses some main characteristics (Spada and Lightbown , 1993) presented in Box 3.2.

Box 3.2   Main characteristics of CLT

(1) The meaning is emphasized over form;
(2) Simplification of the input through the use of contextual props, cues and gestures rather than structural grading (the presentation of one grammatical point at a time in a sequence of form simple to complex linguistics features);
(3) Use of a variety of discourse types introduced by role-playing, stories, real life materials;
(4) Grammar should be learned communicatively;
(5) The amount of correction is kept to a minimum, letting the students express themselves;
(6) Learners should have considerable exposure to the second language speech from the teacher and other learners, and instructors should provide opportunities for learners to play an active role.

(1) The main characteristics of this approach to language teaching (see also Box 3.3) are that the meaning is emphasized over form. Genuine questions (ask questions to which students do not know the answer) as opposed to display questions (type of questions asked to make students display knowledge) are used because there is a focus on meaning rather than form. As Lee (2000:1) has emphasized 'communication need not to be equated with an instructor asking questions and learners answering them. Rather, communication will be defined as the expression, interpretation and negotiation of meaning'. Students and teachers must make some mutual efforts to understand interactions. Pica (1992:200) has defined negotiation of meaning as 'those interactions in which learners and their interlocutors adjust their speech phonologically, lexically and morphosyntactically to resolve difficulties in mutual understanding that impede the course of their communication'. Interactional modifications make input more comprehensible (Lightbown and Spada, 1993). Input should be modified in terms of speaking a simplified language on the part of the teacher so that the learners can understand.

(2) Input is the vital ingredient in SLA. As argued by Krashen (1982) and others (Lee and Van Patten, 1995, 2003; Gass, 1997;) comprehensible and meaning-bearing input promotes acquisition. Simplifications of the input through the use of contextual props, cues and gestures also promote acquisition. Comprehension activities should be used without initial requirements for the students to speak in the target language. The main function of language teaching is to provide comprehensible input (useful especially for beginners and

foreign language learners) which leads to a low filter (high motivation and low anxiety). Little pressure should be exercised for learners to perform at high levels of accuracy and, in the early stages, comprehension is emphasized over production. Classroom activities should be designed to evoke communication and not be wasted in grammatical lectures or manipulative and mechanical exercises.

(3) Learners must be involved in learning tasks which allow them to perform a range of communicative functions with the target L2. CLT should encourage the use of a variety of discourse types tasks (e.g. role-playing, stories, use of authentic materials).

(4) As discussed in the previous chapter, grammar should be learned communicatively. Learners should be provided with communicative tasks that contain enough samples of the linguistic features that learners are trying to learn. Learners must be engaging in communicative tasks where grammar is enhanced using different techniques (e.g. input enhancement, consciousness raising, processing instruction).

(5) The amount of correction in the L2 classroom must be kept to a minimum, as the emphasis must be to allow learners to express themselves. In CLT error correction is seen as having a negative effect on learners in terms of lowering their motivation and attitude. An alternative form of correction might be done by the teacher by repeating what the students have said with the correct form (recasting) or using other forms of corrective feedback such as negative enhancement techniques. Negative enhancement techniques would involve providing learners with some information about the incorrectness of the particular use of a form/structure by enhancing the mistake in different ways (e.g. making a funny face or offering a quizzical look).

(6) Learners should have considerable exposure to the second language speech from the teacher, and other learners and instructors should provide opportunities for learners to play an active role. As indicated by Lee and Van Patten (1995, 2003) the teacher's role in the ALM was to transmit knowledge (authorative transmitter), and the student's role was to receive that knowledge (receptive vessel). With the shift to CLT, teachers interact with the students and encourage them to interact with each other (Larsen-Freeman, 1986; Lee and Van Patten, 1995, 2003). The role of the teacher has to be one of constructing dynamic classroom tasks (architect) and encouraging learners' participation and contribution (resource person or co-builder). To that end, the materials that the teachers use must permit these new roles. Therefore the traditional question/answer task should be supplanted by a task-oriented activity. By providing a series of tasks to complete, tutors play the role of architects

encouraging learners to take responsibility for generating the information themselves rather than just receiving it. The typical example is the traditional open-ended question 'What is your view about the qualities of English and Japanese people?' This is simply a speaking exercise and it is not designed to help learners learning about each other's views or a specific topic (see Lee and Van Patten, 1995). Task-based activities should encourage interaction and participation and learners become active participants (cobuilders) in shaping up the activity.

Question to reflect on . . .

Can you plan a communicative language lesson in Japanese taking into consideration the main characteristics of this approach?

Box 3.3 Communicative language teaching: implications for teaching

(1) Group work is considered essential in the development of Communicative Competence. In group work students are encouraged to negotiate meaning, use a variety of linguistic forms and functions and develop overall fluency skills. This is in contrast to teacher-learned instruction.

(2) Focus on form and focus on meaning activities are desirable.

(3) L2 learners are encouraged to participate (role) in their learning through the task the completion of a task.

(4) L2 learners are encouraged to integrate their skills practice to reflect a more authentic use of language.

(5) Authentic materials should be used wherever possible so that learners will be better prepared to deal with real language outside the classroom setting. On the other hand research in SLA has shown that simplified input increases the learner's ability to comprehend.

Comprehensible input and negotiation of meaning

Input is the primary ingredient for the development of competence (Gass, 1997; Van Patten and William, 2007), and although it might not be sufficient it is certainly necessary for acquisition (Krashen, 1982; N. Ellis, N., 2003). As indicated by Lee and Van Patten (1995) input must be comprehensible and meaning bearing. It must be comprehensible as L2 learners must be able to understand and process the input. It must be meaning bearing input and must have a communicative intent. The question is: How do you make it comprehensible? There are linguistic and non-linguistics techniques to make input more comprehensible for L2 learners. As teachers, we can modify input by simplifying the language so that learners can process more input.

Question to reflect on . . .

How do you make input comprehensible and meaning bearing? Can you think of few examples in Japanese?

We can use different non-linguistics means such as pictures, photos and drawings to modify the input so that learners can comprehend it. How do you make input meaning-bearing? As outlined by Lee and Van Patten (1995, 2003; and Van Patten, 2004) 'communication is about expressing, interpreting and negotiating meaning.' Communicative activities should engage L2 learners in the interpretation, expression and negotiation of meaning as these types of activities will create the optimal conditions for acquisition (see Chapter one). Interactionist theory (Long, 1980; Gass, 1997) recognizes the importance of comprehensible input (Krashen, 1982) but views interactional modifications as crucial in making input comprehensible. Classroom research has proved that more interactional modifications and negotiation take place in paired group activities than teacher fronted activities. Negotiation has been defined by Lee (2000) as 'interactions during which speakers come to terms, reach agreements, make arrangements, solve a problem or settle an issue by conferring or discussing'. In interaction tasks the purpose of language use is to accomplish some tasks not to practice any particular forms. Input will provide the linguistic data necessary to develop a L2 linguistic system and output will help learners to develop the use of the language for communicative purposes.

Ellis (1990) and Van Lier (1988) review theory and research and extrapolate the conditions for the development of communicative competence (see Lee, 2000):

(1) Learners must be receptive to the language and have a need and desire to communicate;
(2) Learners require opportunities to take responsibility in communication;
(3) Learners and instructors must make an effort to be understood (negotiation of meaning);
(4) Learners need opportunities to communicate by performing communicative functions;

Teacher Traditional Role ---- Authoritative ---- Drill leader

Student Traditional Role ---- Note taking ---- Parrot

Teacher New Role ---- Resource Person ---- Information

Gatherer
Negotiator

Student New Role ---- Architect ---- Builder ---- Coworker

Figure 3.2 Roles and tasks (Adapted from Lee and Van Patten (1995:12–16)).

(5) Instructors must provide learners with opportunities to participate in planned and unplanned discourse (similar to outside classroom);
(6) The discourse should contain many samples of the linguistics features that learners are trying to learn.

The role of the teacher and the learner changes in the communicative approach. As indicated in Figure 3.2 (adapted from Lee and Van Patten, 2003) the role of the teacher in the ALM was the one of the person who possesses the knowledge and transmits that knowledge to the learner. Learners are playing a very passive role and are not taking responsibility in this process as argued by Lee and Van Patten (1995, 2003). With the advent of the communicative language teaching approach these roles dramatically change. According to Lee and Van Patten (1995) the teacher is now a 'a resource person' as he prepares the structure of the activity but he is not responsible for its final accomplishment. Learners must take initiative and responsibility to complete the task. The teacher is a 'resource person' as he has the information learners needed to complete the task, but he is only willing to provide this information if learners are also willing to gather the information. A different term used by Lee and Van Patten (1995) for the role of the teacher is 'architect' as the teacher plan a task but learners have to act as 'cobuilders' of that communicative task as they need to take initiatives and make decisions in order to compete the task successfully.

Question to reflect on . . .

Can you think and develop an example of an activity for the teaching of Japanese where both L2 learner and instructor cooperate to build together the activity/task? (see Figure 3.2)

Practical understanding of CLT

There seems to be a clear understanding of what CLT is about, which is accepted in various educational contexts and applied in various ways. According to Richards and Rodgers (1986:83)

> communicative language teaching is best considered an approach rather than a method. Thus although a reasonable degree of theoretical consistency can be discerned at the levels of language and learning theory, at the levels of design and procedure there is much greater [sic] room for individual interpretation and variations than most methods permit.

The fact that this approach is interpreted in different ways is, however, evidence of the confusion that exists in this area. There are, as suggested by Mitchell (1988), as many interpretations and descriptions as there are language teachers. In their review of how Japanese language teachers' view and practice CLT, Sato and Kleinsasser (1999) conclude that teachers develop their own view about CLT, which was not based on the theoretical assumptions and the existing academic literature but directly grounded on their personal ideas and experiences.

Johnson (1982) identified two main approaches within CLT. He calls these two approaches the unificationist and the separationist position. In the first approach (unificationist), instruction has no role to play as teachers should focus on providing learners with communicative and message-orientated practice right from the start (Newmark, 1966; Prabhu, 1987). Learners should be engaged in communicative tasks where they must focus their attention on meaning. In the second approach (separationist), learners should receive instruction that focus on both form and meaning. That is, language-related features are explicitly taught and this is followed by communicative practice. Littlewood (1981, 1992) argues that the ability to 'communicate' involves both an ability to use language systematically and appropriately. Littlewood suggests that a communicative approach cannot mean abandoning the initial emphasis on structure. He proposes a methodological framework in which L2 learners move from 'pre-communicative' to 'communicative activities' (Littlewood, 1981:86). According to Littlewood (1981:85) 'through *precommunicative* activities, the teacher isolates specific elements of knowledge or skill which compose communicative ability, and provides the learners with opportunity to practise them separately'. He argues (1981:86) that 'in *communicative* activities, the learner has to activate and integrate his pre-communicative knowledge and skills, in order to use them for the communication of meanings'.

Despite the debate around some aspects of CLT, almost everybody has agreed that previous approaches to L2 instruction, which focused on the isolated presentation and practice of grammatical rules and error correction, have not been successful. The prevailing view has been that instruction which emphasizes opportunity for learners to communicate ideas, express a greater variety of functions and interact in a more natural and spontaneous way would lead to more successful learning. However, there is empirical and theoretical support that the inclusion of some form of focus instruction is needed in CLT (Spada, 1987).

CLT offers a new dimension in language teaching and learning. If the classroom can become an area of 'co-operative negotiation, joint interpretation and sharing of expression' (Breen and Candlin, 1980), then the teacher gives the students the opportunity for spontaneous production of language in classroom activities (Brumfit, 1984). If all this is combined with the opportunity of making mistakes and teacher tolerance, the students can interact with each other without being afraid of overcorrection. The main point is to create the appropriate conditions in the classroom (see Lee and Van Patten, 1995) in which L2 learners have the opportunity to interact with each other on specific topics. The main contribution of this approach to language teaching is that the primary focus is shifted from the grammatical forms to the communicative properties of the language. This does not mean that accuracy should be sacrificed for the sake of fluency; however, it should not inhibit the natural use of language which takes place in the classroom as students interact. Although, as pointed out, there are different interpretations and theoretical positions of communicative language teaching, these are some general principles shared by professionals that CLT should

- encourage the development of communicative competence through the use of tasks that develop all L2 learners skills;
- take into account learners' needs and should aim at improving their motivation;
- be based on a on notional–functional syllabus which allows for natural learning;
- commit to a message-orientated use of the target language in the classroom.

A communicative teaching model for grammar instruction

Littlewood (1981) argues that the ability to communicate involves both an ability to use language systematically and appropriately. In order to achieve this we cannot abandon the initial emphasis upon structure in a communicative approach, especially if we take into account the constraints of a foreign language context in terms of lack of exposure time and variety of language-generating contexts (and also the way learners process input, see Chapter 1 and 2). Littlewood (1981:1) has argued that 'one of the most characteristics features of communicative language teaching is that it pays systematic attention to functional as well as structural aspects of language.' Based on the theoretical views on the role of formal instruction presented in Chapter 1, classroom-based research findings on the role of different types of grammar teaching and this new CLT philosophy we suggest a two- stage model:

(1) Input stage
(2) Output stage

Input stage

In the first stage, which is the input stage, learners should be exposed to comprehensible and meaning-bearing input. In the case of grammar instruction for instance, learners are exposed to a grammatical feature in the input that they receive (listening to a passage or reading a text). In this way, while learners are listening or reading a text, we want to restructure the input to allow learners to process correctly and efficiently the grammatical items in the input. At this stage, the teacher will provide learners with the opportunity to focus on language items and link one form to one meaning (see structured input activities in Chapter 4).

The output stage

The second stage should provide the learner with the opportunity to practise the linguistics items. Lee (2000:11) has assigned a specific role for output as the role that 'output plays in language development is to push learners to develop communicative language ability'. Input practice pushes learners to connect a particular meaning with a particular form. Our concept for output practice as related to grammar instruction is parallel. Output practice, as part of grammar instruction, should push learners to express a particular meaning via a particular form. Specifically, we advocate the use of structured ouput practices (Lee and Van Patten, 1995, 2003). As previously stated by Lee and Van Patten (1995:121) 'structured output activities have two main characteristics: they involve the exchange of previously unknown information and, they require learners to access a particular form or structure in order to express meaning'.

Lee and Van Patten (2003:154) offer the following guidelines for developing structured output activities:

(1) present one thing a the time
(2) keep meaning in focus
(3) move from sentences to connected discourse
(4) use both written and oral output
(5) others must respond to the content of the output

Question to reflect on . . .

Can you develop a structured output activity in Japanese?

In the output practice, a variety of communicative tasks are used to help learners to practice linguistics items. Linguistics items are contextualized through the use of role-play or an information gap activity. Learners at this stage make authentic and purposeful use of the language.

How would such a model exist in practice? Let's give an example of the implementation of this model in the teaching of Japanese. In the teaching of Japanese communicatively, we would need to take into consideration two pedagogical problems. First of all, Japanese language teaching is still very traditional as it concentrates on imparting knowledge of the language system with very few practical suggestions for developing learners' functional use of the language. Second, teachers of Japanese are not fully aware of the characteristics of CLT and have not been fully trained to teach Japanese communicatively. Considering that instruction should move from input practice to output practice we want to present the following example. The topic of our teaching is 'talking about past events' and the structure is the use of the past tense in Japanese. The topic is chosen because this verbal morphology structure occurs frequently in interaction in daily life and is used in a variety of situations (e.g. talking about your holiday, describing past events).

At input stage (see Activity A) learners are exposed to the grammatical feature (past tense in Japanese) which is enhanced in this case so that learners are helped to notice it in the input. Learners will have to be exposed to a variety of activities which focus on input practice where learners are encouraged to make form-meaning connections (see Chapter 4 for more examples of structured input activities).

Activity A

Read the following sentences describing what your partner did and express you view as to whether it is possible or impossible.

                                                                    Possibile   Impossibile

1) Watashi wa Asa hayaku oki**mashita**
2) Watashi wa Gogaku gakkou ni okurete iki**mashita**
3) Watashi wa Hikouki to Kuruma de ryokou shi**mashita**
4) Watashi wa Nihongo o benkyo shi**mashita**
5) Watashi wa Nihongo o hanashi**mashita**
6) Watashi wa Ohiru gohan o tabe**mashita**
7) Watashi wa tomodachi to Piza o tabe**mashita**
8) Watashi wa Eigakan ni iki**mashita**
9) Watashi wa takusan hataraki**mashita**
10) Watashi wa tomodachi to yoru gohan o tabe**mashita**
11) Watashi wa osoku ne**mashita**
12) Watashi wa Nihon de ichinichi jyu netei**mashita**

Compare your opinion with your partner
It does apply to me   ☐
It does not apply to me   ☐

At output stage, we develop structured output activities which learners would be asked to complete after they have been practising the past tense through structured input activities at input stage. In Activity B, the focus is on one form and one meaning and learners are asked to talk about past events (in this case talk about how they spend their weekend). Learners were asked to use a particular form (past forms in Japanese) to express a particular meaning (how they spend their weekend) and are involved in exchanging previously unknown information and using that information to establish who had the best weekend.

Activity B   Your instructor's weekend

Step 1
You will hear the first part of a sentence about your instructor's week-end. Change the verb in brackets (Japanese present forms) to complete the sentence.

1. Shumatsu watashi wa tomodachi to _____ (sugoshimasu).
2. Watashi wa terebi de totemo ii eiga o _____(mimasu).

(Continued)

Activity B   Your instructor's weekend—Cont'd

3. Watashi wa Paul to kouen o _____ (arukimasu).
4. Watashi wa bar de wain o takusan _____ (nomimasu).
5. Watashi wa totemo ii hon o _____ (yomimasu).

Sentence heard by learner:

1. *Shumatsu watashi wa tomodachi to sugoshimashita.*
2. *Watashi wa terebi de totemo ii eiga o mimashita.*
3. *Watashi wa Paul to kouen o arukimashita.*
4. *Watashi wa bar de wain o takusan nomimashita.*
5. *Watashi wa totemo ii hon o yomimashita.*

Step 2 What did you do at the week-end?
Present your sentences to your partner. Your partner will also present his sentences to you (write them in the chart below).

Myself	My Partner

Step 3 Compare the sentences to find out who had the most interesting week-end!

A follow-up activity at output stage is Activity C. At this stage learners should have internalized the form/structure and we should provide learners with opportunities to use the form/structure to express themselves using their own creativity in increasingly authentic and unpredictable situations. Learners should be provided with activities to converse freely and enthusiastically to convey meaning.

Activity C

Fill the grid below by gathering all the information about how your partners spent Christmas. You need to ask the following information:

Where
Who with
When
How long
How

Step 1

namae	noko ni	dare to	itsu	denogurai	nani de

Step 2 Review the information gathered and present them to your partners with the view of arguing who had the coolest Christmas.

In Activity C, learners are asked, in step 1, to find out what their friends have done during the Christmas holiday using the past tense and filling the grid with the information they gather. In step 2, learners are asked to review the information gathered in order to establish who had the coolest Christmas and why.

Summary

In this chapter, we have presented and discussed the main characteristics of the CLT approach. Teachers of Japanese should take into account characteristics and guidelines required to implement CLT at classroom level. They should do the following:

- Provide learners with opportunities to communicate, exchange information and negotiate meaning;
- Provide learners with opportunities to use a number of communicative functions of the language through communicative tasks;
- Provide learners with opportunities to participate in planned and unplanned discourse activities.

Based on the input processing model, the criticism of traditional grammar instruction and the fact that acquisition is input dependent, we propose a communicative model to grammar teaching that should move from input practice to output practice. Structured input activities should help learners to process grammatical items in the input. Structured output practice should help learners to access these grammatical items in their developing system to create output. This type of practice focuses on meaning, and learners participate in activities where they make output for a specific communicative purpose.

In the following two chapters, we will provide practical suggestions as to how we can incorporate grammar communicative tasks in the teaching of Japanese and how to develop communicative tasks to teach listening, writing, speaking and comprehension skills in Japanese.

More questions to reflect on . . .

(1) Can you summarize the main tenets of this new communicative approach to language teaching?
(2) Can you find in the literature relevant empirical evidence (Japanese studies) in support of this approach to language teaching?
(3) Can you develop a series of communicative activities/task in Japanese where the role of the instructor and the student change?

Key terms

Communicative competence: consists of a series of competences learners would need to develop in a target L2.

Communicative language teaching: this refers to an approach to language teaching based on communication which is defined as the 'expression, interpretation and negotiation of meaning in a given social and situational context' (Van Patten, 2003:115).

Comprehensible input: according to Krashen (1982) input must be modified to make sure that it is comprehended by the learner.

Functional syllabus: it is a communicative syllabus organized on different linguistic functions.

Negotiation of meaning: refers to interactional modifications such as comprehension checks or requests for clarification between instructor and learner or learner and learner during communication.

Further reading

Lee, J. (2000). *Tasks and Communicating in Language Classrooms.* New York: McGraw-Hill.

Lee, J. and Van Patten, B. (1995). *Making Communicative Language Teaching Happen.* New York: McGraw-Hill.

Lee, J. and Van Patten, B. (2003). *Making Communicative Language Teaching Happen,* 2nd ed. New York: McGraw-Hill.

Nunan, D. (2001). *Second Language Teaching and Learning.* Boston, MA: Heinle & Heinle Publishers.

Savignon, S. (2005). *Communicative Competence: Theory and Classroom Practice.* New York: McGraw-Hill.

The Role and Practice of Grammar Teaching: Designing Communicative Grammar Tasks for Teaching Japanese

Chapter Outline

Introduction (Historical perspectives)

Over the past 50 years we have witnessed some dramatic changes (from deductive to inductive approaches to grammar teaching) in the way language is taught in the language classroom. In the grammar translation approach, teachers prioritized the explicit teaching of grammatical rules. The main assumption was that a second language is learned through the deduction of the grammatical properties of a target L2 which would allow learners to develop a conscious and explicit representation of that language. Teachers expectations were for L2 learners to be able to translate texts from L1 to L2 as this ability was seen as the most important knowledge to develop (see Box 4.1).

Box 4.1 Main characteristics of the grammar translation approach

Instruction consists of teaching how to read and translate.
Instruction is not on the target language.
Instruction focuses on translation practice.
Instruction engages learners in structural practice.

The Direct Method proposed a different approach to grammar teaching. According to this method, grammar should be taught inductively. Learners should learn grammar by interpreting contextual and situational cues rather than receiving explicit explanations. Learners should be continuously exposed to the target language (see main characteristics in Box 4.2).

Box 4.2 Main characteristics of the direct method

Instruction is in the target language.
Instruction consists of listening and imitating correct patterns.
Instruction focuses on pattern drill practice.
Instruction follows a chronological order in the development of the four skills (listening-speaking-reading-writing). Listening and speaking is emphasized over reading and writing.

The ALM, based on the habit formation theory, argued that good language habits are learned through the process of repetition, imitation and reinforcement. This method emphasized the use of memorization and pattern drills as described in the previous chapter (see main characteristics if this method in Box 1.1 in Chapter 1).

Box 4.3 Main characteristics of the Cognitive-Code Method

Instruction is synchronized with the cognitive ability of the learner.
Instruction consists of teaching grammar using the L1 and with the help of symbols and graphs.

(Continued)

Box 4.3—Cont'd

Instruction is based on the use of tasks in which learners must substitute and transform grammatical features of the target language.

Instruction is based on the use of tasks in which the practice is contextualized in
a real situation.

The Cognitive-Code Method, influenced by Chomsky (1965), in contrast with the ALM, is a deductive method of teaching grammar that sustains that learners need to understand and analyse L2 grammar in order to build up their linguistic competence. Learners should understand the grammatical system of the L2 rather than merely memorize it (see main characteristics in Box 4.3).

Grammar instruction was relegated to a fragile and peripheral role in Krashen's theory (1982). He sustained that grammar instruction might help learners to monitor their L2 production but does not have any effects on their competence. Long (1983) addressed the question as whether grammar instruction *per se* makes a positive impact on the acquisition of a second language. Long provided some evidence to support the view that instruction makes a difference in terms of being beneficial for adults as well as for children, for intermediate and advanced learners. For Long (1983), the positive effects of instruction can be successfully measured through integrative or discrete-point tests and in acquisition-rich and acquisition-poor environments (i.e. in settings where learners have little opportunity to hear the language outside their language class). In his review, he compared the achievement of learners after a considerable period of classroom instruction, natural exposure and a combination of the two. He concluded that a combination of instruction and exposure to the language was more beneficial than exposure alone, as instruction seems to speed up the acquisition processes.

However, despite Long's view, with the advent of the CLT approach the view around the role of grammar changed again. Heikel and Fotos (2002) have described communicative approaches to language instruction as instruction that does not include formal grammar instruction and the correction of learner errors. The assumption is that grammar instruction does not help learners develop any kind of communicative ability in the L2. In CLT, learners are asked to perform tasks with large quantities of meaning-focused input containing target forms and vocabulary. Spada (1987) carried out an investigation using COLT (Communicative Orientation of Language Teaching, see this observation scheme in Chapter 6), an instrument developed particularly to observe and describe specific communicative aspects of instructional practices and procedures in L2 classroom. Spada (1987) investigated the effects of different implementations of the same highly communicative instructional programme on learners' improvement in competence and proficiency. The evidence provided by Spada suggests that learners make more rapid progress when they experience both a focus on form and a focus on meaning in combination with an overall communicative programme.

There is still a very open debate on the role and the effects of grammar instruction in SLA. Despite the fact that we cannot draw any definite conclusion about its role, we are able to claim today that although the effects of grammar instruction appeared to be limited, grammar instruction might have a facilitative role as outlined in Part A of this book. As affirmed by Lee and Van Patten (1995) it seems that learners have internal mechanisms which organize linguistic data independently of the order, explanation and practice in which the linguistic forms are presented. However, there is empirical evidence which has shown that grammar instruction seems to promote more rapid SLA and to contribute to higher levels of ultimate achievement (Long, 1983; Ellis, R., 1994). Having said that, instruction appears to be constrained. According to Pienemann (1984) instruction will not enable learners to acquire any developmental features out of sequence. Instructors might be successful, as claimed by if learners have reached a stage in the developmental sequence that enables them to process the target structure. The important question seems to be, not whether grammar instruction *per se* makes a difference but whether certain types of grammar instruction techniques/approaches are more effective than others. One of the questions raised by Van Patten (2004) is: how do we teach grammar so that instruction works with acquisition processes and not against them? The language classroom is becoming more and more communicative, however the way grammar is taught has hardly changed at all. As argued by Lee and Van Patten (1995, 2003) the challenge today is not whether or not we should teach grammar but to find a way to incorporate grammar in a communicative framework. The question is: which is the better approach or technique to grammar instruction that can be best incorporated in a CLT programme?

All these questions have been addressed by recent classroom-based research reviewed in Chapter 2. This research has been conducted on one hand to ascertain the role of grammar instruction, and on the other hand to measure the effectiveness of specific approaches and techniques to grammar teaching (see reviews in Doughty and Williams, 1998; Norris and Ortega, 2000; Nassaji and Fotos, 2004).

The role of grammar instruction

There has been a dramatic shift from traditional grammar-oriented methods to more communicative grammar approaches. This shift has meant a change in the way grammar is taught and practised in the language classroom. In traditional methods, grammar was provided through long and elaborated explanations of the grammatical rules of the target language. Paradigms of those grammatical rules were provided and followed by output-based practice (written and oral exercises) where the main focus was to practise the grammatical rules to obtain accuracy. Paulston (1972) has argued that traditional instruction is usually provided following a particular sequence which goes from mechanical to communicative drills practice (see example in Japanese in Activity A).

Activity A

1 下線の部分を過去形に直す練習をしましょう。
   わたしは　ぎんこうに　いきます。

2 あなたのパートナーを見て、質問に答えてください。
   彼は何を着ていますか。
   彼は何をしていますか。
   彼は何を勉強していますか。

3 あなたのパートナーは、暇な時何をしますか、何をしませんか、現在形を使って、尋ねてみてください。

In Japanese language teaching, the way grammar is taught is still very traditional. The grammar translation method was widely used to teach foreign languages in Japan and more recently the use of the audio-lingual methods is spread (use of transformation and substitution drills). Most books used in the United Kingdom to teach Japanese as a foreign language approach the teaching of grammar in a very traditional way. The Grammar section of this book is generally characterized by paradigmatic explanations of linguistic structures and grammatical principles in L1 learners. The paradigmatic explanation is followed by pattern practice and substitution drills. Real life situations are completely ignored and practice is implemented in a completely decontextualized way. Let's take for example the teaching of two adjectives in Japanese -*i*- and -*na*-. The paradigms in Table 4.1 and Table 4.2 introduce learners to this grammatical structure with two tenses: present affirmatives/negatives and modifying forms. The purpose is for learners to memorize the various forms

Table 4.1 I - i adjective: memorize the following –i-adjectives

-i adjectives	Present forms affirmative	Present forms negative	Modifying noun
big	Okii desu	okikunai desu	okii
expensive	takai desu	takakunai desu	takai
good	ii desu	yokunai desu	ii
new, fresh	Atarashii desi	atarashikunai desu	atarashii
small	chiisai desu	chiisakunai desu	chiisai
cheap	yasui desu	yasukunai desu	yasui
bad	warui desu	warukunai desu	warui
old	furui desu	furukunai desu	furui
interesting	omoshiroi desu	omoshirokunai desu	omoshiroi
difficult	mazukashii desu	mazukashikunai desu	mazukashii
far	toi desu	tokunai desu	toi
good, tasty	oishii desu	oishikunai desu	oishii
busy	isogashii desu	isogashikunai desu	isogashii
boring	tsumaranai desu	tsumaranakunai desu	tsumaranai
easy	Yasashii desu	yasashikunai desu	yasashii
near	chikai desu	chikakunai desu	chikai

(Adapted from the text-book *Japanese for Busy People* (pp. 97–98); The Association for Japanese-Language Teaching, 1994, Kodansha America).

Table 4.2 IV - na adjective: memorise the following –na adjectives

-na- adjectives	Present forms affirmative	Present forms negative	Modifying nouns
pretty, clean	kirei desu	kirei dewa arimasen	kireina
Quiet	shizuka desu	shizuka dewa arimasen	shizukana
Famous	yumei desu	yumei dewa arimasen	yumeina
kind, helpful	shinsetsu desu	shinsetsu dewa arimasen	shinsetsuna
Free	hima desu	hima dewa arimasen	himana
Lively	nigiyaka desu	nigiyaka dewa arimasen	nigiyakana
Convenient	benri desu	benri dewa arimasen	benrina
well, healthy	genki desu	genki dewa arimasen	genkina

(Adapted from the text-book *Japanese for Busy People* (p. 99); The Association for Japanese-Language Teaching, 1994, Kodansha America).

before they are asked to practise them through mechanical drills (see Activity B and Activity C.).

The question addressed in this chapter is whether there are types of grammar teaching that could be incorporated successfully in the teaching of Japanese. The theoretical and empirical findings presented in the previous chapters have on one hand indicated the limited role for instruction, and on the other hand highlighted the importance of incorporating grammar in a more communicative framework of language teaching by devising grammar tasks that enhance the grammatical features in the input. The question is to determine what type of grammar is more successful in terms of helping learners internalize the grammatical features of a target language.

Our challenge is to provide an alternative way to introduce the linguistic properties of this language in a communicative framework of language teaching. Despite the fact that Japanese is different from romance languages, and despite the fact that we need to take into consideration that Japanese possess very complex structures, we should develop tasks that introduce learners to patterns of the language not through explanations and memorization (see Table 4.1 and 4.2, from the text-book *Japanese for Busy people* (p. 99)) but rather through exposure and processing of those linguistics features. Rather than using a deductive approach which involves the use of translation we advocate more inductive approaches.

In Chapter 2, we have reviewed studies investigating the effects of using different techniques to enhance grammar in the input and create grammatical tasks that are different from traditional approaches to grammar instruction. In this chapter we will examine how to develop those tasks for teaching Japanese.

Activity B

例ににならって、下線の部分を変える練習をしましょう。
わたしたちは　きれいな　レストランで　しょくじを　しました。

1. しずかな
2. ゆうめいな

Activity C

例にならって下線の部分を変え、対話を作ってください。
はやしさんは　どんなひとですか。
しんせつな　ひとです。

1. おもしろい
2. げんきな

Question to reflect on . . .

What is the role of traditional grammar instruction in Japanese language teaching? Are drills still used? Do you think they have a role?

Input enhancement: designing grammar tasks for teaching Japanese

As repeatedly said, comprehensible and meaning-bearing input is one of the main factors in SLA. Learners must be exposed to comprehensible and meaning-bearing input for acquisition to take place. As Wong (2005:33) has highlighted, there are techniques that would help teachers to expose learners to comprehensible input and positive evidence while at the same time drawing learner's attention to some linguistics properties of the target language. Wong (2005) has identified two main techniques that would help learners notice and possibly acquire a targeted feature: input flood and the textual enhancement techniques. The advantage of input flood is that it provides comprehensible meaning-bearing input. It is also effective as it does not disrupt the flow of communication (Wong, 2005:42). However, as underscored by Wong (2005:43) 'because this technique is so *implicit*, it is difficult for instructors to know whether learners are actually learning anything through the flood.'

Input flood

As Wong (2005:37) has affirmed in input flood

> the input learners received is saturated with the form that we hope learners will notice and possibly acquire. We do not usually highlight the form in any way to drawn attention to it nor do we tell learners to pay attention to the form. We merely saturate the input with the form.

When we design input flood activities, we should follow these guidelines (from Wong, 2005:44):

(a) Grammatical tasks using input flood should either be used in written or oral input.
(b) The input learners receive must be modified so that it contains many instances of the same form/structure.
(c) Input flood must be meaningful and learners must be doing something with the input (i.e. reconstruct a story, draw a picture for instance).

In the case of the particle *ne* in Japanese. This final particle (it comes at the end of a sentence) is used to express the communicative attitude of the speaker towards the listener. In English tag questions such as: isn't it?, don't you?, do you? and you know? are all translated into *ne*. The sentence in Japanese *Kyō wa ii tenki desu ne* means 'It is a nice weather today, isn't it?'. This particle is very frequently used in conversation and it is mainly used by the speaker to ask for the agreement of the listener (like in the previous example). Although comprehensible input is the essential ingredient in SLA, learners do not seem to be exposed to enough input containing the particle *ne* to be able to process this feature. In addition to that, this feature seems to be difficult to acquire (see Ohta, 2001a, 2001b) by beginner learners of Japanese. Empirical research (Ohta 2001a, 2001b) has shown that *ne* is one of the most difficult features to process while at the same time a very frequent feature used in conversation by Japanese native speakers. Despite this, many Japanese language textbooks have not proposed any particular grammatical task to help learners to acquire and use this feature. Learners should be provided with opportunities to notice and acquire *ne* through input enhancement techniques. The purpose of designing input flood activities in this case, is to help learners to be exposed to a greater amount of input (through these techniques) containing the target form which hopefully will allow learners to notice and subsequently acquire this form. In Activity D, oral input is provided to learners of Japanese. The dialogue consists in short-sentences containing many instances of the target item. Learners are familiar with the other grammatical contents of the sentences except for the sentence final particle *ne*.

Activity D

練習　「ね」

ジョン；　きょうは　いい　でんきですね。

たなか；　そうですね。てんきもいいし、あたたかいですね。
　　　　　どこに　いきますか。

ジョン；　トムさんと　すしを　たべにいきます。

たなか；　いいですね。すしは　おいしいですね。
　　　　　トムさんも　すしが　すきだと　いっていましたね。

ジョン；　たなかさんも　いっしょに　いきませんか。

たなか；　そうですね。きょうは　きんようびですね。
　　　　　おなかもすいているし　いきたいですね。
　　　　　でも、ぎんこうに　いかなくてはなりません。

ジョン；　よかったら、あとから　きませんか。

たなか；　じゃ、あとから　いきますね。

A second example of input flood grammar task in Japanese is the acquisition of the *ga sukidesu* (to be fond of . . .) structure. The purpose of Activity E is to help learners to attend the structure in the input. Learners read the story (Activity E) and then are asked some questions by the instructor.

Activity E

練習問題1
下の文章を読んで、下のa)〜 d)の文の内容が正しいか、正しくないか答えてください。

きのうのあさ、アレッサンドロは　テニスをしに　いきました。かれは　テニスを

とても　たのしみました。そのあと、ビールを　1ぱい　のむために　パブに
いきました。

かれは　そのパブで　ともだちと　あい、かれらは、えいがかんに　いくこと
にしました。

パブをでたあと、かれは　じぶんのくるまをとりにいきました。そしてかれら
は

くるまで　えいがかんに　いきました。ところが、かれらは、じこに　あいま
した。

そしてくるまを　つぶしました。
a) アレッサンドロは　テニスを　まいにち　します。
b) アレッサンドロは　でんわで　ともだちを　えいがに　さそいました。
c) アレッサンドロは　ともだちの　くるまを　ぶつけました。
d) アレッサンドロは　のみすぎました。

As pointed out by Wong (2005:43) overall advantages for input flood are:

(1) input flood material can be accommodated easily to any subject in which learners are interested;
(2) the instructor can simply manipulate any materials so that this input contains many uses of a particular target form.

Textual enhancement

Wong (2005:48) has defined textual enhancement as 'the use of typographical cues such as bolding or italics to draw the reader's attention to particular information in a text.' Designing this type of grammar tasks will involve following these guidelines (see Box 4.4 and see list below from Wong, 2005:49):

(a) grammatical tasks using textual enhancement should use written input;
(b) the target form is enhanced visually altering its appearance in the text (i.e. the form can be italicized, bolded or underlined).

In the textual enhancement activity below (see Activity F) the target form is visually altered with a different colour (red) so that it is enhanced in the input.

Activity F　Adapted from Noriko Hikima

練習　　「ね」
ジョン；きょうは　いい　でんきですね。

たなか；そうですね。てんきもいいし、あたたかいですね。
　　　　どこに　いきますか。

ジョン；トムさんと　すしを　たべにいきます。

たなか；いいですね。すしは　おいしいですね。
　　　　トムさんも　すしが　すきだと　いっていましたね。

ジョン；たなかさんも　いっしょに　いきませんか。

たなか；そうですね。きょうは　きんようびですね。
　　　　おなかもすいているし　いきたいですね。
　　　　でも、ぎんこうに　いかなくてはなりません。

ジョン；よかったら、あとから　きませんか。I changed な to ま

たなか；じゃ、あとから　いきますね。

The form has been highlighted in the dialogue with the textual enhancement techniques with the hope that learners will notice it. The advantages of this textual enhancement activity are listed as follows (from Wong, 2005:56):

(1) learners can be exposed to more instances of *ne* and as result of this there are more chances that they will notice the form;
(2) learners will be exposed to meaning-bearing input from this type of tasks;
(3) it is a form of input enhancement that can be easily integrated and it is easy to use.

Consciousness raising: designing grammar tasks for teaching Japanese

According to Sharwood-Smith (1991), making certain features salient in the input might help in drawing the learner's attention to that specific feature. Enhancing the input through different techniques might be sufficient in helping learners paying attention to the formal properties of a targeted language without the need of metalinguistic discussion. Rutherford and Sharwood-Smith (1988) coined the term 'consciousness raising' to refer to external attempts to drawn learners' attention to formal properties of a target language. The goal of this approach is to make learners conscious of the rules that govern the use of particular language forms while it provides the opportunity to engage in meaningful interaction.

As defined by Ellis (1991:236) a CR task 'is pedagogic activity where the learners are provided with L2 data in some form and required to perform some operation on or linguistic property or properties of the target language'.

CR tasks can be inductive or deductive. In the case of an inductive task learners are provided with some language data and are required to provide an explicit representation of the target linguistic feature. In the case of a deductive task, learners are given a description of the target linguistic feature and are required to use that description to apply it to L2 data.

In Activity G (use of present affirmative/negative in Japanese) the CR task has been designed with the following guidelines in mind (see Ellis, 1991):

(a) the task focuses on a source of difficulty for English speaking learners who are learning Japanese;
(b) the data provided is adequate to make learners discover the rule;
(c) the task requires minimal production on the part of the learner;
(d) there is an opportunity for applying the rule to construct a personal statement in order to promote its storage as explicit knowledge.

CR is an approach to grammar teaching (see Box 4.5) in accordance with new views about education as a process of discovery through problem solving tasks. It does not conflict but provide a supplement to the teaching of grammar communicatively.

Box 4.5   Consciousness raising: summary

(1) Identify a particular linguistic feature in Japanese.
(2) Provide learners with an activity in which they have to discover the rule of the target linguistic feature.
(3) Provide learners with a production activity so that they can show their awareness about the target linguistic feature.

Activity G

a) ペアで、下の文を読み、日本語における、非過去の肯定形と否定形のきまりを見つけてください。

    1 わたしは　ともだちと　でかけます。
    2 わたしは　ともだちと　でかけません。

    3 わたしは　テレビを　みます。
    4 わたしは　テレビを　みません。

    5 3じに　バスに　のります。
    6 3じに　バスに　のりません。

b) 日本語の肯定文と否定文のきまりを述べてください。
c) 一週間であなたがいつもすること、しないことを書いてください。

Processing instruction: designing grammar tasks for learning Japanese

In most of the traditional approaches to grammar instruction L2 learners are given an explicit explanation of the rules of a form\structure of a target language, and then they practise these rules through various output exercises. As previously discussed, Paulston's (1972) hierarchy (from mechanical to meaningful drills) reflects the way grammar and practice is still taught in the foreign language classroom. As underscored by Lee and Van Patten (1995, 2003), unlike

TI where the focus of instruction is in the manipulation of the learners' output to effect changes in their developing system, PI aims to change the way input is perceived and processed by language learners. As pointed out earlier, this approach to grammar instruction is consistent with the input processing perspective in SLA. It is therefore evident in Figure 4.2 (adapted form Van Patten, 1996) that PI, in its attempt to alter the way L2 learners process input, should have a greater impact on learners' developing system than an output-based approach to grammar instruction (see Figure 4.1 adapted from Van Patten, 1996) whose aim is to alter how L2 learners produce the target language. Unlike output-based instruction which emphasized grammar rules and oral\written production practice, the purpose of processing instruction is to alter how learners process input and to encourage better form-meaning mapping which results in a grammatically richer intake. In the case of tense markers, processing instruction can make these redundant and non-salient grammatical meaning-form relationships more salient in the learner's input. Given the emphasis on learners' input rather than focusing in on the output, the type of practice provided by the processing instruction approach consists in activities which offer the opportunity to interpret the meaning-form relationship correctly without any practice in producing the targeted form or structure. This is accomplished (as also suggested by Terrell 1991) by providing learners with meaningful input that contains many instances of the same grammatical meaning-form relationship.

This would appear to be a step forward to Sharwood-Smith's position (1993). He suggests a way to provide formal instruction which is based on

Figure 4.1 (Adapted from Van Patten, 1996).

Figure 4.2 Processing instruction (Adapted from Van Patten, 1996).

making some forms more salient in the input so that they come to the learners' attention. PI does this but it also provides opportunities for form-meaning mapping in activities. As outlined by Van Patten (1996:84) 'simply bringing a form to someone's attention is not a guarantee that it gets processed . . . for acquisition to happen the intake must continually provide the developing system with examples of correct form-meaning connections that are the results of input processing'. PI, contrary to 'negative enhancement', does not address the role of output errors since it is solely concerned with the processing of input data. PI might be considered, as mentioned earlier, as a type of 'consciousness-raising'; in the sense that, as indicated by Van Patten (1996:85) it 'does not seek to pour knowledge of any kind into learners' heads; it assists certain processes that can aid the growth of the developing system over time'. However, the ultimate scope of PI is not about raising learners' consciousness about a grammatical form but rather to enrich learners' intake.

PI is a new type of grammar instruction that is concerned with learners' awareness of how grammatical forms and structures are acquired. It is a type of focus on form which draws on the principles of the input processing model (Van Patten, 1996, 2002, 2004). In the model of SLA proposed by Van Patten 'input provides the data, input processing makes (certain) data available for acquisition, other internal mechanisms accommodate data into the system (often triggering some kind of restructuring or a change of internally generated hypotheses) and output helps learners to become communicators and, again, may help them become better processors of input (Van Patten, 2002:760). This new pedagogical approach, based on the input processing model (see Van Patten, 1996, 2002, 2004), seeks to intervene in the processes learners use to get data from the input. Research on input processing has attempted to describe what linguistic data learners attend to during comprehension and which ones they do not attend to, for example what grammatical roles learners assign to nouns or how position in an utterance, influences what gets processed. These processing principles seem to provide an explanation of what learners are doing with input when they are asked to comprehend it. As a result of the way learners attend to input data, Van Patten (1996) has developed a new kind of grammar instruction which guides and focuses learners' attention when they process input. This new type of grammar instruction called PI is diametrically opposed to traditional instruction which consists of drills in which learner output is manipulated and instruction is divorced from meaning or communication. PI is a more effective method for enhancing

Table 4.3 I verbs: memorize the following verbs in their present and past forms

	Present forms		Past forms	
	Affirmative	Negative	Affirmative	Negative
go	ikimasu	ikimasen	ikimashita	ikimasendeshita
come	kimasu	kimasen	kimashita	kimasendeshita
return	kaerimasu	kaerimasen	kaerimashita	kaerimasendeshita

(Adapted from the text-book *Japanese for Busy People* (p. 56); The Association for Japanese-Language Teaching, 1994, Kodansha America).

language acquisition as it is used to ensure that learners' focal attention during processing is directed towards the relevant grammatical items and not elsewhere in the sentence. Its main objective is to help learners to circumvent the strategies used by them to derive intake data by making them to rely exclusively on form and structure to derive meaning from input.

As repeatedly said, PI is the most promising approach to language grammar teaching. The way grammar is approached and practiced in Japanese textbooks is through the use of paradigmatic explanation and pattern practice which usually follow the following order: memorization of patterns, transformation and substitution tasks. If we look at the way Japanese past forms are introduced (see Table 4.3 from the text-book *Japanese for Busy people* (p. 56)) learners are asked to memorize some verbs in the present and past forms.

After they have memorized the forms they are engaged in practising those forms by changing a pattern accurately and appropriately (see example below from text-book *Japanese for Busy People* (p. 56)).

II Practice the following cy changing the underlined part as in the example given.
ex. [Watashi wa] Ginkō ni ikimasu.

1. kaisha
2. Amerika

III Make dialogues by changing the underlined part as in the example given.
A ex. Q: [Anata wa] Ashita kaisha ni ikimasu ka.

Aa: Hai, ikimasu.
An: Iie, ikimasen.

(Continued)

Cont'd

1. tomodachi no uchi
2. depāto
3. taishikan

B ex. Q: Kono <u>densha</u> wa Tokyō Eki ni ikimasu ka.

Aa: Hai, ikimasu
An: Iie, ikimasen.

1. basu
2. chikatetsu

PI is a different approach to grammar instruction and grammar practice, diametrically different than the more traditional approach described above. PI consists of three main components (see also Box 4.6):

(1) Learners are given explicit information about a linguistic structure or form (see example below).
(2) Learners are given information on a particular processing principle that may negatively affect their picking up of the form or structure during comprehension (see example below).
(3) Learners are pushed to process the form or structure during activities in which the input is manipulated in particular ways to push learners to become dependent on form to get meaning.

Explicit information on the use of present and past tense

Japanese sentences end with the verb. The endings of verbs show the tense. You must pay attention to the end of the verb to establish when the action took place.

> Past form: Senshu Kyoto ni ikimashita
> Present form: Maishu Kyoto ni ikimasu

Information about the processing principle

Do not rely on the temporal adverb to understand when the action takes place. You must pay attention to the tense ending to understand when the action takes place. In the case of describing past events pay attention to the ending of the verb: -*mashita*.

In the case of describing habitual and present events pay attention to the ending of the verb: -*masu*.

After receiving the explicit information about the targeted linguistic feature and the information about the processing principle affecting that feature, learners are pushed to process the form or structure through structured input activities (SIA). In SIA, the input is manipulated in particular ways to push learners to become dependent on form and structure to get meaning. As outlined by Wong (2004a), PI 'pushes learners to abandon their inefficient processing strategies for more optimal ones so that better form-meaning connections are made' (p. 35). As the main component of PI, SIA help learners to make those form-meaning connections.

Lee and Van Patten (1995:104; see also Farley, 2005) have produced the following guidelines for SIA:

(1) Present one thing at a time.
(2) Keep meaning in focus.
(3) Move from sentences to connected discourse.
(4) Use both oral and written input.
(5) Have the learner 'do something' with the input.
(6) Keep the learner's processing strategies in mind.

(1) Paradigms and rules should be broken down into smaller parts and taught one at the time during the course of the lesson. Students are presented with the linguistic feature before being exposed to SIA. In fact, the type of input L2 learners receive in PI is meaningful as it should help them to make correct form– meaning connections.

(2) Learners should be encouraged to make form-meaning connections through structured input activities. As pointed out by Van Patten (1996:68) 'if meaning is absent or if learners do not have to pay attention to meaning to complete the activity, then there is no[*sic*] enhancement of input processing.'

(3) Learners must be engaged in processing the input sentences and must respond to the input sentence in some way through referential and affective types of SIA.

(4) SIA which combines oral and written input should be used as some learners respond better to one than the other. This is in order to account for individual differences.

(5) SIA should be designed to make learners do something with the input they receive (i.e. agreeing or disagreeing). During SIA activities learners should

be encouraged to make form-meaning connections. Learners must be engaged in processing the input sentences and must respond to the input sentence in some way.

(6) Learners' attention should be guided not to rely on natural processing strategies. Activities in which the input is structured to alter learners' reliance on one particular processing principle should be created.

Referential activities are those for which there is a right or wrong answer and for which the learner must rely on the targeted grammatical form to get meaning. Affective structured input activities are those in which learners express an opinion, belief, or some other affective response and are engaged in processing information about the real world.

In the referential Activity H, learners must process the input to determine whether the statement they hear is referring to a present or past action. Learners are obliged to attend to the grammatical markers (present vs. past in Japanese). Considering that learners are affected by the Lexical Preference Principle (P1d.) temporal adverbs for past and present were removed from the input sentences so that students were forced to attend to the past or present tense forms to encode the meaning.

Activity H

練習問題 1
今から聞く文の内容は、いつ行われたことですか。去年か毎年行われることか。
正しいほうにしるしをつけてください。

1 きょねん　　　　まいとし
2 きょねん　　　　まいとし
3 きょねん　　　　まいとし
4 きょねん　　　　まいとし
5 きょねん　　　　まいとし
6 きょねん　　　　まいとし
7 きょねん　　　　まいとし

問題文
1 イタリアに行きました。
2 イタリアに行きます。
3 テニスをしました。
4 テニスをします。
5 いい映画を見ました。
6 ポールとはなしました。
7 ポールとはなします。

In affective Activity I, learners must attend to sentences containing the past tense in Japanese and they are asked to express their views about whether they think that the statements are possible or impossible.

Activity I

練習問題 2
下の文を読み、文の内容は学生にとってよくあることか、そうでないことか、あなたはどう思いますか。

よくある　めったとない

1　わたしは あさはやく おきます。
2　わたしは ごがくがっこうに おくれて いきました。
3　わたしは ひこうきと くるまで りょこうしました。
4　わたしは にほんごを べんきょうしました
5　わたしは にほんごを はなしました。
6　わたしは おひるごはんを たべました。
7　わたしは ともだちと ピザをたべました。
8　わたしは えいがかんに いきました。
9　わたしは たくさん はたらきました。
10　わたしは ともだちと よるごはんを たべました。
11　わたしは おそく ねました。
12　わたしは にほんで いちにちじゅう ねていました。

In referential Activity J, learners attention is directed to the final part of the sentences learners heard. This is because they can establish whether the sentence is affirmative or negative.

Activity J

練習問題 3
今から聞く文の内容は肯定文でしょうか、それとも否定文でしょうか答えてください。文の最後を注意して聞いてください。

1　肯定　　　否定
2　肯定　　　否定
3　肯定　　　否定
4　肯定　　　否定
5　肯定　　　否定

問題文
1　私はイタリア語を勉強します
2　私はイタリア語を勉強しません。
3　私はロンドンに住みます。
4　私はロンドンに住みません。
5　私は劇場に行きません。

In affective Activity K, learners are asked to pay attention to the end of the sentence to establish whether it is a positive or negative sentence and then they must agree or disagree with those statements.

Activity K

練習問題 4

学生の日課についての文を読みますから聞いてください。

それぞれの文は、肯定文でしょうか、それとも否定文でしょうか答えてください。

次に、あなたは、それぞれの文の内容はよくあることですか、そうではないことですか。

	肯定	否定	よくある (usual)	めったとない (unusual)
1				
2				
3				

問題文

1 私は友達と出かけます。

2 私は友達と出かけません。

3 私は劇場に行きます。

Activity L

絵と文を見て正しい順番に並べなさい。それらはアレッサンドロさんの日本での休暇です。きおつけて、1枚写真がたりません。どんな絵でしょうか。

わたしは　にほんに　いきました。

わたしは　とうきょうに　いきました。

わたしは　ひこうきで　いきました。

わたしは　にほんの　しょくじを　しました。

わたしは　ロンドンに　かえりました。

わたしは　さけを　のみました。

わたしは　きょうとに　いきました。

In referential Activity L, learners must look at the pictures and the sentences containing the linguistic target feature (namely past tense in Japanese) and must put them in a chronological order.

Activities H, I, J, K and L are activities developed to teach L1 English speakers learning Japanese in the United Kingdom.

Box 4.6   Processing instruction: summary

(1) Identify a particular linguistic feature in Japanese that is affected by one of the processing principles.
(2) Provide L2 learners with information about the linguistic feature and the processing problem.
(3) Engage L2 learners in structured input activities.

In current traditional approaches to grammar instruction teachers and textbooks tend to provide a paradigmatic visualization and explanation of the forms (see Figure 4.1 and Figure 4.2 for examples). This is follow by pattern practice (written or oral) of the targeted form (see below an example from *Japanese for busy people*, p. 98).

II Practice the following patters by changing the underlined parts in the examples given.

A. ex. Kono kamera wa ōkii desu.

Ano kamera wa chiisai desu.

1. kono kuruma, ano kuruma
2. kono tanago, ano tamago

III Make dialogues by changing the underlined part as in the example given.

A. ex. Q: Nihon-go wa yasashii desu ka.

Aa: Hai, yasashii desu.
An: Iie, yasashikunai desu.

1. muzukashii
2. omoshiroi

This type of traditional and mechanical practice does not take into account and address any of the factors and variables affecting learners when they are acquiring an L2. PI does take into account many of those factors (limited capacity of attention and processing and other psycholinguistics constraints in the acquisition of the grammatical properties of an L2) and provide a different approach to grammar teaching. We propose an approach to grammar

Activity M (Structured input activity)

日本語の文をきいて、肯定か,否定か ☑ してください。あなたはその意見に賛成
ですか、反対ですか。

Please check whether the sentence that you are about to hear are either
affirmative or negative. Check if you agree or disagree about the statement.
(Tokyo = Tokyo, the name of the city nihon jin = Japanese)

1. Aff. ☐	Neg	☐	Agree	☐	Disagree ☐
2. Aff. ☐	Neg	☐	Agree	☐	Disagree ☐.
3. Aff. ☐	Neg	☐	Agree	☐	Disagree ☐.
4. Aff. ☐	Neg	☐	Agree	☐	Disagree ☐.
5. Aff. ☐	Neg	☐	Agree	☐	Disagree ☐.

The sentence that learner hear;

1. Tokyo wa nigiyaka desu	東京はにぎやかです。	Tokyo is lively
2. Tokyo wa okii desu	東京はおおきいです。	Tokyo is big
3. nihon jin wa shinsetu desu	日本人はしんせつです。	Japanese are kind
4. nihon jin wa ookiku nai desu	日本人はおおきくないです。	Japanese are not big
5. nihon jin wa nigiyaka desu	日本人はにぎやかです。	Japanese are not lively

Adapted from Kuri Komatsu

Activity N (Structured output activity)

1) 次のロンドンについての意見について、あなたは賛成ですか反対ですか。
Indicate if you agree with these statements shown below about London. You
can add your own statement as well if you wish

		賛成 agree	反対 disagree
1. London wa takai desu	ロンドンはたかいです。	☐	☐
2. London wa nigiyaka desu	ロンドンはにぎやかです。	☐	☐
3. London wa benri desu	ロンドンべんりです。	☐	☐
4. Igirisujin ha ookikunai desu	イギリス人はおおきくないです。 ☐		☐
5. Igirisujin wa shinsetu desu	イギリス人はしんせつです	☐	☐

2) 上のロンドンについての意見から、あなたの質問、意見を考えてクラス
メートに聞いてみてください。（例：東京について、日本について、あな
の国について）
Using the idea as we have seen in 1), create the questions (statements) to ask
your friends in the classroom. (ex: about Tokyo, Japan, people, or your country)

3) あなたの意見とクラスメートの意見をまとめ、クラスで発表してください。
Prepare your opinion and your friends' opinion about your statements and
conclusion to present in your classroom.

Adapted from Kuri Komatsu

instruction that moves from structured input activities to structured output activities (see Activity N and guidelines to develop this type of activities in Chapter 3 of this book). In Activity M, the task is structured so that L2 learners must pay attention to the Japanese Adjective-*i* and *-na* in order to complete the activity.

Summary

Input is the main and most important ingredient in SLA. As highlighted by Van Patten and Williams (2007) it is necessary, but it might not be sufficient. Learners might benefit from a type of focus on form that helps them to notice and then process forms in the input they are exposed to. Input enhancement techniques, consciousness raising tasks and structure input practice might help learners to acquire an L2 language. These techniques might facilitate and speed up the way languages are learned and are an effective way and a non-traditional approach to incorporate grammar teaching and grammar tasks in communicative language teaching. Input enhancement provides foreign language learners with access to comprehensible input, positive evidence and helps L2 learners to pay attention to grammatical forms in the input. CR tasks help learners to pay attention to grammatical forms in the input while at the same time provide the necessary input learners need to acquire an L2. Processing instruction and structure input practice help learners to process input correctly and efficiently and therefore increase learners intake and provide right information for learners' developing system.

In this chapter we have principally highlighted two modules to incorporate the teaching of grammar in Japanese in a communicative context. In the first module, we advocate the use of implicit techniques such as input flood or input enhancement to enhance the opportunities for learners to notice those forms/structures in the input.

In the second module, we advocate that the use of structured input activities which would enrich learners' intake and consequently have an impact on their output. This input practice (structured input) should be followed by output practice in the form of structured output activity practice.

More questions to reflect on . . .

(1) Can you underline the main characteristics of the input enhancement techniques and provide more examples for Japanese grammar teaching?
(2) Can you underline the main characteristics of consciousness raising tasks and provide more examples for Japanese grammar teaching?

(3) Can you underline the main characteristics of processing instruction and provide more examples for Japanese grammar teaching?

(4) Can you focus on a grammatical feature in Japanese and provide an example of one structured input activity and one structured output activity?

Key terms

Direct method: a method where the emphasis is on using the target language at all times in the classroom and focus on developing listening and speaking skills.

Grammar translation method: a very traditional method which is based on grammatical analysis and translation.

Cognitive code method: a method that supports the view that learners need to analyse the grammatical features (analysis and problem solving) of the targeted language in order to develop their competence.

Drills (substitution and transformation): refers to an activity that focuses on a linguistic element.

Explicit information: consists of information provided to the L2 learners about the formal properties of an L2 target language.

Input flood: refers to provision of many instances of the same form/structure in the input L2 learners receive.

Textual enhancement: refers to the technique of highlighting forms in a written text to increase saliency of the target form.

Structured input activities (referential and affective): refers to an activity developed in order to help learners to process efficiently and accurately the input they are exposed to.

Further reading

Ellis, R. (1997). *SLA Research and Language Teaching*. Oxford: OUP.

Farley, A. (2005). *Structured Input: Grammar Instruction for the Acquisition-Oriented Classroom*. New York: McGraw-Hill.

Lee, J. and Benati, A. (2009). *Grammar Acquisition and Processing Instruction*. Clevedon: Multilingual Matters.

Van Patten, B. (1996). *Input Processing and Grammar Instruction*. Norwood, NJ: Ablex.

Wong, W. (2005). *Input Enhancement: From Theory and Research to the Classroom*. New York: McGraw-Hill.

Designing Communicative Tasks in Teaching Japanese

5

Chapter Outline

Introduction

The communicative approach was the result of growing dissatisfaction with the ALM and the grammar-translation methods in language instruction. In traditional approaches to language teaching, L2 learners were not exposed to real everyday language and as a result of this they did not know how to communicate using appropriate social language, gestures or expressions. The CLT approach makes use of real-life situations that necessitate communication. The teacher sets up a situation that students are likely to encounter in real life. Unlike ALM which relies on repetition and drills, the communicative approach engages learners in communicative tasks that need to be accomplished for a communicative purpose. The real-life simulations change from day to day. Students' motivation to learn comes from their desire to communicate in meaningful ways about meaningful topics. Instructors in communicative classrooms take less control and act as facilitators of students' learning (Larsen-Freeman, 1986). Instructors set up the task and monitor the development of that task as learners take a more proactive role. Littlewood (1981:19) argues that 'while learners are performing, the teacher can monitor their strengths and weaknesses.' Because of the increased responsibility to participate, students may find they gain confidence in using the target language in general. Students are more responsible managers of their own learning (Larsen-Freeman, 1986).

In order to accomplish the aims of this new and innovative approach to language teaching, the role of teacher and learners in CLT has changed as indicated by Lee and Van Patten (1995, 2003) and Nunan (2001). The teacher is assuming a new role of resource person or architect whereas the learner is undertaking a more active role where he is encouraged to use language more creatively through communicative tasks (Lee and Van Patten, 1995, 2003, have discussed the role of students and teachers in CLT).

In Activity A, we present an example in teaching Japanese where the teacher is taking the role as an 'architect' (Lee and Van Patten, 1995:14) of the task. The teacher is responsible for designing the task but is not responsible for the final product as learners take the role of 'builders' (Lee and Van Patten, 1995:16) of the task itself. Learners are engaged in a step by step task in which they are active participants. They must make a list of the different negative aspects of smoking. Then, they need to compare their views and finally they are asked to do something with the information they have gathered and draw a chart about the danger of smoking. This type of activity represents as highlighted by Lee and Van Patten (1995:16) 'a multilayered communicative event, that is, an interaction requiring various steps and tasks'. In Activity B, instead, learners are simply asked to talk about the topic of 'smoking'. Lee and Van Patten

Activity A

1. たばこ の 悪い 影響 をパートナー と 一緒 に リストにしてください。
2. あなた の 作った リスト を 他 の グループ の 人 と 比べてください。
   あなた は 全部 同意 しますか
3. 他 の 生徒 とたばこ の 悪い 影響 を 表 に してください。

Activity B

たばこ は 有害です。　あなた は たばこ を すうこと が 危険だと 思いますか。

(1995:15) called this type of activity (Activity B) 'an open-ended discussion question'. According to Lee and Van Patten, this activity is only designed to give the opportunity for learners to speak and it is not 'designed to learn about the topic and from each other'.

The way language is taught has changed over the years as discussed in previous chapters. These changes have affected various aspects of learning and teaching. In ALM, language was seen as very hierarchical rule-based system where learners acquire the language by forming good habits and avoiding bad habits. The main objective for learning is to master forms and structures of the targeted L2 in a graded syllabus of phonology, morphology and syntax. In many text-books used for teaching Japanese, grammar is provided at the beginning of the lesson with the help of paradigms.

They are given a paradigmatic explanation of the forms and asked to memorize all the forms. This will have negative effects on learners as they will be overloaded with information and they will feel unmotivated. The explicit and paradigmatic explanation is usually followed by a series of exercises (mechanical drills) focusing on the grammatical item that has been introduced. This mechanical practice consists of pattern practice and substitution drills where real life situations are completely ignored. Usually after the use of drills (pattern practice), repetition and memorization of the targeted forms/structures, learners are provided with short dialogues in romanized Japanese based on the key sentences which is followed by a translation exercise. The teacher's role in all these activities is central as he provides an inflexible model for practice and he controls the direction and the pace. Learners are simply following instructions in order to produce the forms/structures correctly. Their role is clearly a passive role as they are only asked to produce correct responses. This type of practice reflects a very teacher-centred classroom type of practice.

With the advent of CLT, this method is challenged as language is seen as a system for the expression of meaning. The primary learners' function is to communicate a message to their peers. As a result of that, the focus is on meaningful activities that promote real communication. Learners must be engaged in communicative tasks where they use language that is meaningful. The syllabus should include structures, functions, notions and tasks which might reflect learners' need to communicate. All communicative activities must engage learners in sharing information, negotiating meaning and interacting with others. In this way the role of teachers will change as teachers will act as a facilitator of the communication process while at the same time learners will act as negotiator and interact throughout the tasks. The task-based activities advocated by CLT must be developed with the intention to promote communication and communicative language use.

As defined by Lee (2000:32)

> a task is (1) a classroom activity or exercise that has (a) an objective attainable only by the interaction among participants, (b) a mechanism for structuring and sequencing interaction, and (c) a focus on meaning exchange; (2) a language learning endeavour that requires learners to comprehend, manipulate and/or produce the target language as they perform some set of work plans.

Ohta (2001a) has claimed that despite the fact that CLT had an influence on Japanese language teaching, the teaching of Japanese is still very traditional and based on a very structural syllabus. However, communicative approaches are becoming very popular in Japanese language teaching and teachers are developing activities that provide more communicative practice. Despite the fact that we should be cautious in applying findings on L2 research and guidelines in communicative language teaching to the teaching of Japanese, as Japanese is different from any other romance and non-romance language, we would like to provide some general guidelines that could be easily applied to make practice more communicative.

In the following four paragraphs we will look at examples and provide general guidelines as to how to develop communicative tasks that will help learners improve listening, speaking, reading and writing skills in Japanese. These general guidelines have been developed and discussed by Lee and Van Patten (1995, 2003).

Developing listening/comprehension communicative tasks

The role of comprehensible input and conversational interaction has assumed greater importance in second language teaching. Krashen (1982), Gass (1997) and Long (1996) have emphasized the benefits for the use and role of comprehensible input, conversational interaction and negotiated interaction in the language classroom.

Nakakubo (1997) argued that providing Japanese learners with simplified input in listening comprehension tests facilitates comprehension and increases the rate and quality of learning. Considering that input is seen as a vital ingredient for acquisition, listening as a skill has acquired an important role in the language classroom.

Listening is not just a bottom-up process where learners hear sounds and need to decode those sounds from the smaller units to large texts, but it is also, as argued by Nunan (2001:201) a top-down process where learners reconstruct 'the original meaning of the speaker using incoming sounds as clues. In this reconstruction process, the listener uses prior knowledge of the context and situation within which the listening takes place to make sense of what he or she hears'. Lee and Van Patten (1993, 2005) argue that listening is an active and productive skill and they embrace the Wolvin and Coakley (1985) model which emphasizes that listeners must be active participants during listening comprehension activities. According to Wolvin and Coakley listeners use a series of mental processes and prior knowledge sources to understand and interpret what they hear. Wolvin and Coakley (1985) support the view that listening is a very active skill given that learners are actively engaged in different processes while they are exposed to aural stimuli. Wolvin and Coakley distinguish between three main processes (see Lee and Van Patten, 1995:60):

perceiving;
attending;
assigning meaning.

As highlighted by Lee and Van Patten (1995:60) 'perceiving refers to the physiological aspects of listening.' Attending requires an 'active concentration by the listener'. Assigning meaning involves 'personal, cultural and linguistic matters interacting in complex ways'. The lesson to learn from these views according to Nunan (2001:203) is that ' it is important, not only to teach bottom-up processing skills such as the ability to discriminate between minimal parts, but it is also important to help learners use what they already know to understand what they hear.' Lee and Van Patten (1995) distinguish between various types of listening tasks and this is on the basis of the following factors:

(a) role of learners and tasks;
(b) learners strategies.

(a) In everyday life people engage in a variety of situations during which they listen. In developing classroom listening task we need to take into consideration two types: collaborative or reciprocal listening; non-collaborative or nonreciprocal listening. Collaborative or reciprocal tasks involve an exchange between two people and negotiation of meaning on both parts (the speaker and the listener). In non-collaborative or nonreciprocal tasks there is no negotiation of meaning and the listener is only an observant (this is often the scenario in language classrooms). According to Rost (1990) listeners play an important role in constructing the discourse.

(b) The listener must be given opportunities to reflect on their learning processes and can be equipped with a range of learning strategies. These strategies as highlighted by Nunan (2001:219) would include the ability to listen for specific information, gist or a specific purpose, inferencing and personalizing. Learners must be aware of what they are doing and what the activity is trying to achieve.

Now if we look at listening in the language classroom the two main questions to be asked are (see Lee and Van Patten, 1995:66): What kind of listening tasks are learners engaged in the classroom? Do they have the opportunity to develop their skills and strategies?

Learners are generally engaged in listening tasks that are collaborative and non-collaborative (particularly in the language laboratory). The challenge is to develop listening task which will stimulate the development of listening skills while equipping them with listening strategies. As Littlewood argued (1981:67) 'the nature of listening comprehension means that the learner should be encouraged to engage in an active process of listening for meanings, using not only the linguistic cues but also his metalinguistic knowledge.'

According to Lee and Van Patten (1995) learners can begin to develop listening skills if instructors take the following steps to (adapted from Lee and Van Patten, 1995:68)

(1) expose listeners to comprehensible input;
(2) use the target language to conduct business;
(3) allow learners to nominate topics and structure the discourse. Learners are much more likely to get involved and become active listener and participant;
(4) develop a listening task for a specific communicative purpose;
(5) respond to learner as a listener, not an instructor. That is, as a listener the instructor should engage in appropriate listening performance. In this way, learners see and hear how to perform as listeners in the second language;

(6) provide some good listening gambits to learners. In addition to simply allowing more opportunities for collaborative listening, instructors can also point out to learners' typical listening gambits for signalling non-understanding, confirmation, and so forth.

In Activity C, learners of Japanese are given a listening task developed with the intent of closing the gap between the listening test and the learner. In step 1, the purpose of the activity is to activate the knowledge readers will need to possess in order to understand the message conveyed in the text. In step 2, learners are asked to understand elements and parts of the text.

Activity C

聴解問題
ジョン ；　　　今朝は元気。
バーナデット ；きのう眠れなくて、全然気分がよくないわ。
ジョン ；　　　ひどそうだけど、なにがあったんだい。
バーナデット ；変な夢をみたの。
ジョン ；　　　それって、いい夢、いやな夢。
バーナデット ；いい夢でも悪い夢でもないわ、ただ変なの。私が荒れ果てた街
　　　　　　　を歩いていた時、赤くて長い帽子をかぶった男を見たの。彼は
　　　　　　　近づいて 来て、私に笑いかけ、鍵をくれたの。
　　　　　　　突然車の扉が開
　　　　　　　き、私はその車に乗り、走りさったの。車を運転している間、
　　　　　　　外の電気の光が明るすぎて、何も見えなかったわ。
　　　　　　　でも幸い眼鏡
　　　　　　　を車の中でみつけたの。ブレーキが利かなくて、車が
　　　　　　　止まらなかったんだけど、突然止まったの。車を降りたら噴水
　　　　　　　が見えたの。
　　　　　　　その噴水に近づいていくと、そこから水が出ているのではなく、
　　　　　　　音楽が
　　　　　　　出ていることに気がついたの。
ジョン ；　　　なんだって。
バーナデット ；そうなの、音楽だったの。
ジョン ；　　　ところできのう、騒がしくなかった。
バーナデット ；いいえ、何かあったの。
ジョン ；　　　近所の人がパーティーをして、夜間ずっと音楽をかけて踊って
　　　　　　　いたから。

どのような嫌な夢をみたことがありますか。
嫌な夢と悪夢の違いは何ですか。
嫌な夢を見たことがありますか。

練習問題1
カップル2人が夢の話をしているのを聞いてください。それは嫌な夢でしたか、
いい夢でしたか。

(Continued)

Activity C—Cont'd

下のどの言葉がその夢の中ででてきましたか。
赤い車
眼鏡
水
黒い帽子
女性達
水
砂漠
男
鍵

練習問題２
もう一度本文を聞いて、下の絵を話の順番に並べてください。

Question to reflect on . . .

Look at listening comprehension Activity C. Can you think of an additional activity in Japanese?

Littelewood (1981:68) has discussed and presented different types of listening comprehension activities that will help learners to develop their listening skills. Performing physical tasks and transferring information are very common listening tasks in text-book. In the case of 'performing physical tasks' learners might be asked to identify specific information in the message they hear. Learners can be asked to focus their attention on specific features by scanning the aural text for specific information (see Activity D).

With transferring information listening tasks, learners not only have to extract some meaningful information from the text but also need to transfer (e.g. filling a table, completing a chart) some specific information in order to complete the task (see Activity E and F).

Activity D   (Performing physical tasks)

話を聞いて、その話にあう絵を順に並べなさい。

内容

去年の夏、休暇で日本に行った。それはすばらしい休暇だった。私たちは東京に飛び立ち、一週間東京に滞在した。その後、富士山を見に行き、そして京都へ行った。私たちはもう一週間、海のそばに滞在した。私たちは8月中の2週間を日本で過ごした。

14 – 28

Activity E   (Transferring information)

情報転移

電車案内を聞いて、下の表を埋めなさい。

1　次の東京行きの列車はプラットフォーム 3 から 10 時に出発し、11 時半に東京に到着いたします。
2　次の京都行きはプラットフォーム 2 にただいま到着し、9 時に出発いたします。所要時間は 3 時間です。
3　次の東京へ到着する大阪行きの列車はプラットフォーム7 から 16 時に出発し、大阪に 18 時に到着いたします。

目的地	出発	到着	プラットフォーム
	9:00		
東京			
		18:00	

Activity F   (Transferring information)

田中さんの生活と家族のことを表した文の一節を聞き、下の表をできるだけその情報で埋めなさい。

田中氏は１９６０年に日本で生まれたが、ロンドンに住んでいて、グリニッジで働いている。
彼には２人の娘と１８歳の息子がいる。息子は一番年上で、双子の娘より１０年前に生まれている。彼の妻は５歳年下で、イギリス人だ。田中氏は１９８９年以来、日本語の講師としてグリニッジ大学で働いている。

(Continued)

Activity F—Cont'd

国籍	居住地	年齢	職種とその期間	息子と娘の年齢	妻の国籍	妻の年齢

Question to reflect on . . .

Can you think of an additional listening activity in Japanese following Littlewood typology?

Developing oral communicative tasks

In the previous chapters of this book, we have argued that instruction should move from input practice to output practice. Acquisition is intake dependent and instructors would need to provide learners with opportunities in the input they are exposed to, to make correct form–meaning connections. Once learners have hopefully internalized forms and made those form–meaning mappings (through structured input activities or other communicative grammar tasks and not through drills or pattern practice) and the linguistics situation in which the language makes use of these form–meaning connections, we should provide opportunity for L2 learners to use the target language for communicative purpose. Van Patten (2003) has defined output as the language produced by learners that has a communicative purpose and it is produced for a specific meaning. Oral communicative practice is in antithesis with traditional oral practice largely used in traditional text-book. In traditional oral tasks, learners are asked to look at some pictures or a dialogue and then perform that dialogue following a specific pattern (a typical task/exercise is: look at the pictures and practice the following patterns in Japanese). Another form of traditional oral task which is normally found in language text-books is to ask L2 learners to talk about a topic (e.g. describe a friend or a member of your family or talk about your weekend...) without taking into consideration the main principles of the communication act.

As described by Savignon (2005) and emphasized by Lee and Van Patten (1995:148), the communication act involves 'the expression, interpretation and negotiation of meaning' in a given context. Assuming that the context is the classroom, we must create classroom activities that stimulate communication in the language classroom. These activities are called by Lee and Van Patten (1995) as 'information–exchange tasks'. Lee and Van Patten (1995:156) have proposed some guidelines to be used to develop these types of activities such as

(1) identification of a topic;
(2) design an appropriate and immediate purpose;
(3) identify the information source.

(1) First of all, when deciding what type of activity we should develop, we must establish a topic that is familiar, appropriate, interesting and relevant

---

Activity G

練習問題 1
クリスマスに何をしたか、友達と話し合ってください。

練習問題 2
Step 1 クラスの人に下の内容にそって話を聞いて表を完成させてください。
　　　　クリスマス、どこで、だれと、料理、おもしろい話

1　年前
2　年前
3　年前

Step 2 あなたがクラスの人から聞いたクリスマスの話とあなたのクリスマス
　　　　を比べ、比較
　　　　し、短い作文を書いてください。

Namae	Doko ni	Dare to	Itsu	Donogurai	Nani de	Tabemono	Kaimono

(related to every-day life) to the language. In the case of Activity G (adapted from Lee and Van Patten, 1995, 2003), the topic is holiday and birthday celebrations. In designing 'information–exchange tasks' two main points must be kept in mind: level of learner; linguistic demands of the task.

(2) In designing a task, we must make sure that learners collect data through production speech activities for a specific purpose. In Activity G learners are given a questionnaire in order to find out what their friends would like to do over the holiday. In Activity G, learners must complete the table in order to gather some information about their friend's (e.g. filling a table or answering questions) birthday celebrations.

The main purpose of 'information-exchange tasks' is not just about getting or exchanging information but also to do something with the information gathered. L2 learners must have a specific reason for obtaining information and be guided in what to do with the information they have collected.

(3) The purpose of the task would clarify the information source required. In the case of Activity G the information source is learners' personal experience.

Another example of an exchange information task (adapted from Lee, 2000) is Activity H.

Activity H

1. あなたのパートナーと、それぞれの動作は、静かな動作か活発な動作か、述べてください。あなたとパートナーの意見が同じであることが必要です。

	しずかなどうさ	かっぱつなどうさ
パーティーでおどる	☐	☐
バイクにのる	☐	☐
テレビゲームであそぶ	☐	☐
スポーツをする	☐	☐
ほんをよむ	☐	☐
テレビをみる	☐	☐
てがみをかく	☐	☐
しょくじをつくる	☐	☐

この分類わけに他のクラスの人も同意しますか。

2. あなたとパートナーで、他に３つの静かな動作または活発な動作の文を付け加えなさい。

	しずかなどうさ	かっぱつなどうさ
	☐	☐
	☐	☐
	☐	☐

3. パートナーに先週何をしたか聞いて、ステップ４で必要なので、覚えていてください。

4. パートナーの答えを、ステップ１，２で分類したのと比べ、そして下のどれに当てはまりますか。

とてもしずか　　　　　　どちらともいえない　　　　　　とてもかっぱつ

　　1　　　　　2　　　　　　3　　　　　4　　　　5

5. それぞれの行動に対してのあなたの評価をもとに、クラスの表を作ってください。クラス全体の先週の行動はどうだったでしょうか。

Lee and Van Patten (1995, 2003) have suggested that we should move from structured input activities (see Chapter 4) to structured output activities (see activities I and J below) when we aim at practising grammar. Both activities follow the guidelines provided by Lee and Van Patten(2003:154, 1995:121) to

(1) present one thing at a time;
(2) keep meaning in focus;
(3) move from sentences to connected discourse;
(4) use both written and oral output;
(5) others must respond to the content of the output.

Learners of Japanese should be involved in the exchange of previously unknown information while at the same time use and produce a particular target form or structure to express meaning.

Activity I

1. あなたの家族にとって下記のそれぞれの行動はよくあることか、あまりないことでしょうか。
   ほかにもなにか付け加えたいことがありますか。

   　　　　　　　　　　　　　　　　　　よくある　　　　あまりない

   1. みかけたときに だきしめあう
   2. みかけたときに キスしあう
   3. よく でんわを かけあう
   4. おたがいを たすけあう
   5. おたがいをよく りかいしている

2. ステップ１のアイデアを使ってインタビューの為のクラスメイトへの質問を考えてそしてインタビューしてください。

3. ステップ１，２のアイデアを使って、あなたの家族とパートナーの家族のすることを比べ、報告書を作ってください。それをクラスのみんなに報告しあい、あなたの結論を出してください。

Activity J

1. 先生の休暇について、文の最初の部分を聞き、かっこの中の動詞を正しく
変え、文を完成させなさい。

1. _____ 両親を訪ねました。
2. _____ くるまをぶつけました。

1. かれはイタリアにいきました
2. かれはイタリアにいました。

2. どのように休暇を過ごしたか、最低５つの文を下の表に書きなさい。
パートナーとお互いの書いたものを見せ合い、パートナーのも下の表に書
きなさい。

自分	友達

3. 文を比べあい、だれが一番たのしい休暇をすごしたか見つけてなさい。

Question to reflect on . . .

Look at the oral tasks presented so far. Can you think of an additional activity in Japanese?

Developing role plays tasks

Littlewood (1981:49) has pointed out that 'in looking for ways of creating more varied form of interaction in the classroom, teachers of foreign languages (like their colleagues in mother-tongue teaching) have turned increasingly to the field of simulation and, within that field, especially role-playing'. Role-playing is a technique which is essentially a form of simulation where learners are involved in gathering, exchanging information and communicating efficiently. As indicated by Littlewood (1981:51) there is a typology as far as role-playing is concerned. The so-called 'cued dialogues' (see example below) allow learners to interact with each other to convey a specific message. Although it is a quite controlled task as learners are asked to use specific language to communicate, they need to listen and understand their partner in order to respond.

Cued Dialogue

カードを読んでロールプレーを始めなさい。返答する前にパートナーの言っていることを確認しなさい。

Player A	Player B
A: 友達に会って、「こんにちは」と 言う	**B:** 友達を見て、元気か尋ねる
A:「元気です」と言う	**B:** 友達を飲みに誘う
A: 誘いを受ける	**B:** 満足を表現する

You can develop another form of cued-dialogue with additional information as in the example below. Learners need to gather some information for a specific communicative purpose (e.g. book a room, decide on the price, gathering information to make a decision). The result is that learners are assuming greater responsibility to convey a message and gather the information required. There is less control from the teacher, and learners are asked to become more creative.

Cued dialogue with additional information

キューダイアローグと追加の情報

Role Play A

あなたは東京にいます。そしてホテルの部屋をを探しています。一泊、シャワーとお風呂付の一人部屋が必要です。値段と他にホテルにどんな設備があるかを尋ねることが必要です。

Role Play B

あなたはホテルで働いています。二人部屋は空いていません。一人部屋にはシャワーとお風呂どちらも付いています。すべての部屋にテレビがあります。一泊15000円で朝食付きです。ホテルにはプールとサウナ付きのジムがあります。

In the next example of role-playing with situation and goals as Littlewood (1981:56) suggests 'learners are initially aware only of the overall situation and their own goal in it. They must negotiate their interaction itself as it unfolds, each partner responding spontaneously to other's communicative acts and strategies'.

In the example below learners are giving a role card designed to encourage L2 learners to manipulate the language in the input in a very creative way. The framework of this role-play would facilitate the skimming and scanning of the cards. Each card is divided into four parts: background, start, core, end (see Benati and Peressini, 1998). The background part is to provide both players with the background and set up the scene. The starting part is to help learners to begin the action and be aware of social conventions. The core part is to provide suggestions and to direct the interaction. The suggestions in brackets are there to stimulate thinking so that learners can develop their own ideas for their interaction (see below how to implement the role play in the language classroom) and also given the opportunity to improvise in a real communication task.

Role playing with situation and goals

ロールプレーと状況と目的

Role A (At the Bar)

背景：あなたはイギリス人の学生です。そして日本のビールをパブで飲んでいます。（あなた　は日本のビールが大好きです）夜9時、日本人と思われるほかの学生がパブに入って来ます。

始まり：日本人学生の注意を引き、自己紹介しなさい。ビールを勧めなさい。

核心：会話を続け、次の質問をしなさい（氏名、国籍、学科、、、）。他のの学生の質問を聞く（あなたの週末の予定、、、）

終わり：時計を見て、行かなければならないと説明し、さようならと言う。

Role B (At the Bar) バーにて

背景：あなたはロンドンにいる日本人学生で、英語を勉強しています。今、夜9時で、日本のビールを飲めればいいなとパブに入る。

始まり：あなたに近づいて来る学生に、こんにちはと言う。

核心：自己紹介をし、尋ねられた質問に答える（名前、国籍、学科、、、）そして質問をする（学生の週末の予定）。学生にジョンのことを知っているか尋ねる、もし必要だったらジョンの特徴を述べる。

終わり：さようならと言う

このロールプレーは下記のように使用されるべきだ。

段階1（準備）：学習者は準備するために別々のロールカードを与えられる。(相手のカードを見てはいけない)。この準備は即時応答供給の重圧なしで、創造力と正確さの向上を助けるだろう。

段階2（演技）：学習者はペアで目標言語で交流する。この段階では予期しない状況への対応への機会を提供するだけではなく、学習者の聞き取り、話し方の流暢さを向上させる。

段階3（報告）：学習者のやる気と文化的意識を高めることを強化するだけでは

なく、目標言語の使用に反映するように、学習者の出来栄えに対してフィードバックが与えられるべきだ。

As Littlewood (1981:51) argues role-plays 'gives the interaction some of the uncertainty and spontaneity involved in real communication.'

Question to reflect on . . .

Can you develop one more activity/task in Japanese for each of the following:?
Cued dialogue
Cued dialogue with additional information
Role playing with situation and goals

Functional communicative tasks

Littlewood (1981:22) has identified four types of functional communication activities:

(1) sharing information with restricted cooperation;
(2) sharing information with unrestricted cooperation;
(3) sharing and processing information;
(4) processing information.

As indicated by Littlewood (1981:22) 'the principle underlying functional communication activities is that the teacher structures the situation so that learners have to overcome an information gap or solve a problem.'

In the first type (1) of Littlewood's communicative tasks tipology learners must share and exchange some basic information, through interaction, in order to complete the task. Tasks can be designed so that one learner has to interact with another learner to discover some missing information.

In the second type (2) of functional communication task presented by Littlewood, learners are allowed to interact without restriction in order to solve the problem and complete the task. In both types of tasks, learners must share information to complete the task.

As explained by Littlewood (1982:33) in the third (3) and fourth (4) type of functional communication activities he proposed, these activities 'work on the "jigsaw" principle: each learner in pair or group possesses information which is unique to him: he must share it with others; together, the different pieces of information provide the material for solving a particular problem'. Learners are not only asked to share information but also to discuss and evaluate specific information to complete the task.

Developing reading communicative tasks

Japanese is different from romance languages in that reading in Japanese is made more complicated by Japanese writing unique features. As argued by Chikamatsu (2003:187) 'Japanese writing system does not involve only one type of orthography. Japanese involves both logographic and alphabetic orthographies. Logographic kanji does not have any systematic sound-letter correspondence, and this make reading challenging for L2 Japanese readers.' Similarly the development of listening skills, reading skills are affected by two types of processing: bottom-up and top-down processing. The bottom-up approach consists of the ability for the reader to decode the linguistics information (e.g. orthographic knowledge, lexical (kanji) and syntactic knowledge) in a written text in a gradual way: from the small to large units. Readers will process letters and characters, and analyse and interpret the meaning words and sentences. Top-down processing will involve processing beyond the analysis of linguistics information (e.g. knowledge of text structure, prior knowledge (topics familiarity, culture awareness)).

The so-called Schema Theory (Lee and Van Patten, 1995, 2003) suggests that as learners, our knowledge impacts on how we process and understand new incoming information. As argued by Nunan (2001:257) 'the basic principle behind schema theory is that texts themselves, whether spoken or written, do not carry meaning; rather they provide signposts, or clues to be utilized by listeners or readers in reconstructing the original meaning of speakers or writers.' Some research into the development of reading skills has yielded very interesting results. Minaminosono (1997) conducted a study investigating reading behaviours in intermediate and advanced learners of Japanese. Despite the fact that the results of this study showed that advanced L2 learners of Japanese rely less on bottom-up strategies than poor readers, bottom-up strategies play overall a much more important role in the development of reading skills among L2 Japanese learners than top-down strategies.

Japanese second language researchers have undertaken research on bottom-up processing in L2 Japanese reading. They generally found that L2 learners of Japanese, even at advanced level, rely mostly on bottom-up processing (Everson and Kuriya, 1999). Research findings on reading Japanese texts by foreign learners have shown that pre reading activities are extremely useful in activating the Schema (Chikamatsu, 2003). Among the main pedagogical implications from research in L2 Japanese reading (see Chikamatsu, 2003) are:

- Pre reading activities are very effective to improve schema activation and use of reading strategies;
- Reading should be done for a real-life specific purpose;
- Learners should be asked to perform tasks based on information learned through their reading.

The pedagogical implication of the Schema Theory is the understanding that reading is an interactive process between readers, and texts and readers must associate elements in a text with their pre reading knowledge (Rumelhart, 1980).

Reading activities in traditional text-books consist mainly of two types: translation tasks (read a passage and translate into Japanese); answer questions from a text (a typical task/exercise is: Read the dialogue/text and answer the following questions). Reading should be viewed, as claimed by Van Patten and Lee (1995:189), as 'reading in another language rather than as an exercise in translation'. The fact that language learners do not necessarily have the verbal virtuosity of a native reader means instructors need to use some strategies to help them. The framework presented here takes into consideration the need to guide learners in their comprehension of a text.

The three main steps (see Lee and Van Patten, 1995:199–211) that need to be undertaken in a reading comprehension activity are

(A) preparation
(B) guided interaction
(C) assimilation

Our intention is to develop a reading activity to teach Japanese using the model presented by Lee and Van Patten (1995, 2003).

(A) Pre reading activities must be included to improve the activation of learners' existing knowledge. In order to prepare the learners and activate the knowledge which is relevant to a particular text we want to present and use, many techniques are available. Some of these have been highlighted by Lee and Van Patten (1995:199–204):

• brainstorming as a whole class exercise or in pairs. This can take place before reading the text and should help to bridge the gap between the reader and a text;

- titles, headings and illustrations can be exploited as a means to activate learners' background knowledge;
- scanning for specific information can be used in the case of a text that does not need extensive preparation. We could ask learners to scan the text for specific information that will activate appropriate knowledge.

In Activity K, step 1, learners are asked to read the title of the text and based on that to write down some of the issues they expect to find in the text. This is to activate readers' knowledge that will be needed to use to understand the information in the text. This is an attempt to bridge the gap between the readers and the text.

(B) This is the phase where learners explore the content of a text. We should provide a guide to this process so as to avoid learners reading word for word. This phase consists of a combination of two types of tasks (Lee and Van Patten, 1995:204):

- management strategies in which we suggest ways to divide a text and divide it into small parts;
- comprehension checks implemented during the guided interaction phase so that readers are monitored in an ongoing way.

In step 2 of Activity K, readers are asked to read the text quickly and check whether they have discovered some of the details and issues covered in this text.

In step 3, learners are asked to interact with the text by exploring part or section of the text.

(C) In the assimilation phase the learners are given a series of tasks in which they organize the information in the text (see Lee and Van Patten, 1995:207).

Step 4 of Activity K, is designed to check and verify comprehension. The purpose of this activity is to encourage readers to learn from what they have read.

Activity K

Text

どうしてもたばこをやめたかったから・・・

日本政府がたばこをやめたい人への援助を行っている。

たばこの害をよく知っているにもかかわらず、喫煙者はその悪習から抜け出すことができない。しかしながら、仕事場、駅の構内や病院のような公共の場だ

けでなく、家庭においても、禁煙の規則を適用する場が増加の一途をたどっている。たばこに火をつけられる場所がどんどんかぎられてきている。それでも頑固な喫煙者はその習慣から抜け出せない。たとえ不名誉にも、おろかものだとか優柔不断と呼ばれても喫煙をおもいとどまらない。

しかし現在、日本政府は喫煙者がたばこをやめるためのプログラムにかかわっている。2000年度から始まる禁煙サポートプログラムは、どのようにこの習慣から能率的に抜け出せるかをアドバイスする場を提供することがねらいである。

たばこの危険性が日本に広まって以来、喫煙は下り坂である。その他の喫煙が減っている要因は、喫煙に反感を持つ社会的傾向の増加にある。禁煙タクシーが現れた1988年以来

電車や飛行機、公共の施設、会社でも、たばこを禁止することが広がった。この反喫煙姿勢はたくさんの家庭の中にも根付くようになり、お父さんがたばこに火をつけようとすると、家族はお父さんを家の外にだそうとする。このような好意的ではない環境でも、たばこ愛好者達はニコチンの極楽を容赦なく追い求め、お手洗いで隠れてとか、玄関にでて、たばこの煙をくゆらせている。喫煙者達は、自分たちがつねにバルコニーやテラスにおいだされることに気がついている。

1999年春に行われた厚生省の調査によると、日本の喫煙者の割合はまだ高く、男52.8%,女13.4%である。しかしながら、26.7%の喫煙者がやめたい、37.5%が本数を減らしたいと言っている。喫煙者がたばこをやめたいおもな理由は、健康に悪いからで、80%以上の人がそう思っている。沢山の喫煙者がやめたいがやめられないというのが現状である。

なぜ禁煙がそう難しいのであろうか。たばこは習慣性があり、ニコチンを含んでいるだけでなく、たばこを口にくわえること、手にすることが自然の動作となってしまっている。

強度な中毒者には専門的な助けが必要かもしれないが、ほんの少数の医者のみがその治療を提供し、ほんの少しの援助が政府機構から提供されているのみである。そこで今、厚生省はたばこをやめたい人が、それぞれに必要なガイダンスを受けるための援助をもっと簡単に受けられるようにすることを決めた。

厚生省は、喫煙を心臓発作や脳卒中だけではなく、肺癌、胃癌を含む様々な癌の要因になる恐れがあると列挙している。

1995年の厚生省の推定によると、日本では喫煙に関連した病気が、毎年95,000人の死をもたらしている。喫煙習慣の認可は、健康を死に曝す危険を引き起こす。厚生省は、社会に喫煙がそのように危険であるという意識をたかめることを迅速に計画し、さらに喫煙をやめられる治療ができる専門家を養成することと公共のヘルスセンターを作ると表明している。

Preparation

Step 1　下のタイトルを読んで、文中から考えられる問題点を書きだしてください。

　　1
　　2

Step 2　本文をさっと読み、その中にどのような話と問題点が含まれているか見つけてくだ
　　　　さい。

(Continued)

Activity K—Cont'd

Guided interaction

Step 3　下に書かれた意見は、本文で言われていることに照らし合わせ正しいでしょうか、
　　　　　間違っているでしょうか。

　　　　　　　　　　　　　　　　正しい　　　　　間違っている

1　喫煙者数は減少している。
2　女性の方が男性よりたばこを吸っている。
3　喫煙者は家でだけたばこを吸っている。
4　日本人は皆、たばこの危険性を完全に意識している。
5　厚生省は喫煙に対して事前に対策をとっている。

Assimilation

Step 4　下の1〜3の項目に関して、パートナーと意見を交換してください。
1　喫煙の危険性
2　可能な原因
3　問題解決の糸口

あなたの意見をクラスの他のグループの人と話し合ってください。

Question to reflect on . . .

Look at reading and comprehension Activity K. Can you think of an additional activity in Japanese?

Developing writing communicative tasks

As outlined by Lee and Van Patten (1995, 2003) researchers in composition have emphasized the importance of composing processes. As highlighted by Lee and Van Patten (1995:216), Flowers and Hayes (1981) have argued that writing is a cognitive process that involves a series of sub-processes. Writing is a process where learners explore, consolidate and develop rhetorical objectives.

The same definition used for communication is applicable to the written language. We express ourselves both in speaking and in writing. When we write a grocery list we accomplish an act of communication (Lee and Van Patten, 1995:215). The most famous cognitive process theory of writing is the one put forward by Flower and Hayes (1981). Their model develops around three main components (see Lee and Van Patten, 1995:216):

(1) task environment (the title can constrain the content of a paper);
(2) learner's memory (refers to the long-term memory the writer possesses);
(3) writing processes (i.e. planning, translating, reviewing, monitoring).

Kingawa (1993) carried out a study with learners studying Japanese at intermediate level. This study supported Flower and Hayes's model (1981) as the findings showed that although different L1 (the participants were native speakers of different L1) might have in impact on how L2 learners of Japanese develop writing skills, overall the study showed that all learners of Japanese use planning, writing and reviewing extensively as strategies for writing.

Another study (Hatasa and Soeda, 2001; and see also Hatasa, 2003) which investigated the importance of composing processing in writing among advanced L2 learners of Japanese, also provides some support to Flower and Hayes's model. The findings of this study showed that the L1 and L2 writing processes are very similar and L2 learners rely on planning and evaluation in their composition.

The Flower and Hayes's model presents the different set of thoughts and processes writers engage in while writing. Lee and Van Patten (1995:222) propose an approach to language writing ('composing-oriented activities') which is based on the Flower and Hayes model. This approach consists of two main phases (in Lee and Van Patten: 1995:222):

• pre writing activities in which learners are given different options so that they can make a choice and decide on the direction of their composition;
• writing phase which begins when the preparatory phase is over.

The following is a sample of the various steps (from Lee and Van Patten, 1995:222) used in developing a composing activity from the pre writing phase to the writing phase:

Step 1. Instructor assigns one topic to students in groups;
Step 2. Each group has an amount of time to make a list of ideas related to that topic;
Step 3. Each group should copy the lists from the other groups to be used later in writing;
Step 4. Take your outline and list of ideas and write your composition. You should write a draft of the work and let it sit sometime. You should ask yourself two questions: Are these still the ideas I want to include? Does the order in which the ideas are presented help get my message across? If the answer is no, you should rewrite the composition.

Activity L is an example of how we can develop writing activities following Lee and Van Patten' model (1995, 2003).

Activity L

練習問題1
あなたの死刑に対する意見を短い作文にしてください。

練習問題2
あなたは死刑についてどう思いますか。
それは予防の役割をはたしていますか。
死刑の代わりは何ですか。

練習問題3
Step 1　ペアで下のトピックに関連した考えをリストにしてください。
　　　　死刑の役割
　　　　賛成か反対か
　　　　あなたの国での死刑の位置付け
　　　　死刑に代わるもの

Step 2　それぞれのトピックに関連したあなたの意見をクラス全体に報告してください。

Step 3　どういう読者に対して書くか考えてください。
　　　　学校新聞に
　　　　政府の誰かに
　　　　あなたの同僚に

Step 4　一つトピックを選び、あなたの個人的な意見を含めどんな情報を書きたいですか。

Step 5　あなたの作文の概略をパートナーに見せ、意見を交換し、アイディアをふくらませてください。

Step 6　誰に対して書くか、あなたの概略を心に留めて作文を書いてください。3つの質問
　　　　をあなた自身に問いかけてみることが必要です。

　　　　1　わたしの作文にはっきり自分の考えを示しているか。
　　　　2　文の組み立ては、読者か私の考えを理解する助けをしてるか。
　　　　3　作文の中の文体はふさわしいか。

Question to reflect on . . .

Look at written Activity I. Can you think of an additional activity in Japanese?

Summary

In this chapter, we have provided some practical suggestions for developing L2 learners' communicative language abilities by focusing on classroom communication and interaction. Our main purpose was to offer alternative and more communicative techniques to the teaching of listening, speaking, reading and writing skills in Japanese.

The results of classroom research in second language acquisition briefly reviewed in previous chapters have revealed the limited role of explicit and formal instruction. However, in a communicative approach we should not renounce the teaching of grammar and we should develop less implicit approaches to grammar instruction. Grammar instruction is traditionally taught through this sequence: explanation + drill + output practice. To challenge the traditional approach to grammar teaching we have examined in Chapter 4 a type of grammar instruction called processing instruction.

This type of grammar instruction takes into consideration the way learners process input and offers opportunities for learners to make better form meaning connections. Structured output activities should follow structured input activities.

One particularly important part of communicative language teaching is to help students to develop the ability to listen for a specific purpose. In order to develop learners' listening skills, instructors should provide some tasks which reflect listening situations occurring outside the classroom. Learners should be guided to the task of listening in terms of what meanings they should expect from the passage. However, as in the case of communicative tasks they must be able (take responsibility) to extract the main content/information from the text.

Our goal in the classroom is not to make L2 learners practise language but to make them use the language to obtain information and then perform some kind of communicative act with the information they have gathered. For this particular reason, we have presented 'information-exchange tasks' as a communicative oral task. Role plays can be used to recreate everyday situations and give L2 learners the opportunity to interact with each other. Communicative tasks will allow learners to interact in communicative situations, express real language, develop communicative skills and express their own opinion.

Reading is also an important component of a communicative classroom. However we have proposed a reading comprehension framework which has challenged the way reading is done in traditional approaches (translation and answering questions). In a communicative approach, we take into account the processes responsible for reading comprehension and should develop a step by step approach (from pre reading to personalization).

For writing we have described a similar step-by step approach (pre writing to writing).

More questions to reflect on . . .

(1) Can you compare communicative oral tasks with traditional tasks and provide an example?

(2) Can you compare communicative reading tasks with traditional tasks and provide an example?

(3) Can you compare grammar output communicative tasks (e.g. structured output activities) with traditional instruction output tasks and provide an example?

Key terms

Listening comprehension communicative tasks: we presented communicative tasks for listening comprehension based on the understanding that L2 learners must be motivated communicatively.

Oral communicative tasks: we presented and described exchange information tasks (Lee and Van Patten, 1995, 2003) as oral communicative tasks which stimulate communication in the language classroom.

Reading comprehension communicative tasks: we presented and described reading comprehension activities (Lee and Van Patten, 1995, 2003) based on an interactional framework between the reader and the text.

Role play tasks: we presented different simulation techniques (Littlewood, 1981) to promote interaction in the language classroom.

Structure output activities: output-based practice which would allow L2 learners to exchange previously unknown information while at the same time focus on a particular target form or structure to express meaning.

Writing communicative tasks: we presented and described composing-oriented activities (Lee and Van Patten, 1995, 2003) as communicative tasks to L2 writing which involves a step by step approach to writing (Prewriting phase is followed by the writing phase).

Further reading

Lee, J. (2000a). *Tasks and Communicating in Language Classrooms.* New York: McGraw-Hill.

Lee, J. and Van Patten, B. (1995). *Making Communicative Language Teaching Happen.* New York: McGraw-Hill.

Lee, J. and Van Patten, B. (2003). *Making Communicative Language Teaching Happen,* 2nd ed. New York: McGraw-Hill.

Nunan, D. (2001). *Second Language Teaching and Learning.* Boston, MA: Heinle & Heinle Publishers.

Omaggio Hadley, A.(2001). *Teaching Language in Context,* 3rd ed. Boston, MA: Heinle & Heinle.

Savignon, S. (2005). *Communicative Competence: Theory and Classroom Practice.* New York: McGraw-Hill.

Part C
Classroom Research

In Chapter 6 of Part C of this book the 'experimental methodology' used in classroom research will be presented with the view of encouraging teachers and researchers to undertake classroom studies to investigate Japanese language learning and teaching. Findings from classroom-based research investigating the role of grammar teaching in the acquisition of Japanese will be presented in Chapter 7.

The Experimental Methodology

Chapter Outline

Introduction

Before examining in detail the main components of the experimental methodology, we must stress that second language research has very often a theoretical and an applied scope. In the so-called 'applied research' approach (Nunan, 1992) the researcher is interested in verifying the effectiveness of a theory. The researcher might be interested in investigating a particular theory in second language to look at practical implications for language teaching. At the same time, findings from classroom-based research could lead to a revision of second language theories. Let us consider, for example, an experiment that investigates and compares the effectiveness of different language teaching methods or techniques. Although the main aim of this experiment will be to establish which method or technique is more effective, the results from this experimental research would be of interest to theoreticians since a particular theory might predict that using a particular method would be more effective than another.

Chaudron (1988) identified four main traditions in second language research:

psychometric tradition;
interaction analysis tradition;
discourse analysis tradition;
ethnographic tradition.

The interaction analysis tradition is based on the analysis and observation of classroom interaction in terms of social meanings. It utilizes various instruments and observation systems for coding classroom interactions. The discourse analysis tradition aims at, from a linguistic perspective, fully analysing classroom discourse through studies of classroom transcripts. The ethnographic tradition seeks to study the classroom as a cultural system through naturalistic observation and description.

The psychometric tradition generally aims at investigating and determining language gains from different methods, techniques or materials through the use of the an experimental method. This approach was first applied in large-scale method comparison studies (Sherer and Wertheimer, 1964). In these studies, students were randomly assigned to groups. The experimental groups were taught through an innovative teaching method and the control groups through a 'traditional multiple approach method'. The groups were then tested at the end of the experimental period. Despite the fact that usually some differences between groups were found through achievement tests, the results of this type of study are difficult to interpret as little control was used in establishing what exactly went on inside the classroom. There was no instrument to provide a systematic observation to describe classroom practices in detail, and there was no control as far as the characteristics of the population is concerned. Therefore, it was difficult to know in what way the classes were different from each other. Even if the groups were found to perform differently on certain measures, it was very difficult to establish to what to attribute these differences. Long (1980) called for a more precise description of specific instructional procedures in studies examining the relationship between instructional input and learning outcomes.

Small-scale method comparison studies were carried out with the intention of isolating and comparing the effects of smaller units of instruction on learning. Although these studies were very valuable, they produced inconclusive results. The language teaching process cannot be restricted to the description of a particular method or technique. Other factors (linguistic, sociological and psychological) play their part and contribute to the complex series of interactions which take place in the classroom.

Allwright (1988:196) has pointed out that

> 'it is necessary to find out what actually happens in language classes, not assuming that all that happens is that a particular method or a particular technique is simply implemented, but assuming that something below the level of technique, something less pedagogical takes place.'

Larsen-Freeman and Long (1991) have claimed that in order to promote experimental research in the area of teaching methodologies, future research should focus on more local practices. Another main requirement, pointed out by Spada (1990), is that, experimental research design should include both process (what is actually happening in the classroom) and product (what the learning outcomes are) with an observation component built in to verify the implementation of a particular method or technique. A final requirement is that experimental research should be theoretically motivated in order to present a coherent view of the language teaching and language learning process. The psychometric tradition is quantitative in its approach as it is concerned with product outcomes. Its methods and instruments involve numerical measurement and statistical analysis. However, despite the goal of this approach, a process dimension (classroom observation instrument) should be built into the experimental design to give a better account of the teaching and learning process.

Second language research is carried out for different purposes and is generated from different sources. Sometimes we are driven to research through reading an interesting article or through our own personal interest in a theory for which we intend to collect some support to prove its effectiveness. Other times our common sense and our personal interest guides us into research.

Box 6.1   Why instructors carry out research

- To monitor and influence the direction of new developments.
- To try to find out what is actually going on, recognizing that what actually occurs is not always the same as what is thought to occur.
- To evaluate what is already taking place.

Whatever the reason we are driven to conduct research (see Box 6.1 and Box 6.2), research could be described as a scientific enquiry comprising different components. Overall research contains the following basic components (Nunan, 1992):

(a) an attempt to investigate a behaviour which is not clearly understood;
(b) an observation of that behaviour;
(c) some possible explanations about that behaviour are suggested;
(d) one possible explanation is considered the right one;
(e) more data are collected to test initial hypotheses/questions formulated to investigate that behaviour.

Box 6.2   Where does research come from?

• Published materials (books, chapters in books, articles, report, conference paper, dissertation)
• Personal/Professional interest

The minimal definition of research (Seliger and Shohamy, 1989) is that it is a systematic and scientific process of enquiry. The main aim of any research project is to obtain results which would provide evidence to support or reject the research question or hypothesis of a study (see Box 6.3). The results must be objectively valid and obtained using scientific methods. The research process involves different stages such as defining a problem, stating an objective and formulating a hypothesis. It also involves gathering information, classification, analysis and interpretation to see to what extent the initial objective has been achieved, or supports a specific theory. Research is carried out to solve problems, to verify the application of theories which might lead to new insights, to prove or disprove theories or practical methods or to discover the cause of a problem and find the solution.

Box 6.3   Why read

• At the beginning of your research, to check what other research has been done, to focus your ideas, explore the context for your project.
• During your research, to keep up-to-date with developments, to help understand better the methods you are using, and the field you are researching.
• At the end of your research, to see what impact your own work has had and to help develop ideas for further projects.

Experimental research: characteristics and components

One of the essential characteristics of experimental classroom-based research is that the researchers must control and manipulate various conditions which might be the factors determining the events in which they are interested. Experiments involve manipulation and control of the various variables and factors. Most of the time an experiment will be characterized by manipulating or changing one or more variables and observing the effect of that change on another variable. As stressed by Seliger and Shohamy (1989:10), generally experimental research consists of at least three components:

(1) an initial question/hypothesis generated from previous research;
(2) a procedure to collect data;
(3) a procedure to analyse and interpret the data collected.

(1) A question or a hypothesis. In order to carry out any type of investigation we need to clarify what we want to investigate or identify in a specific research problem which needs a solution or further investigation. We formulate a question or a hypothesis as a result of a review of the current state-of-the-art of a particular research area. We need to identify a problem that needs to be solved.

(2) In order to attempt to answer the research question or hypothesis some form/procedure of data collection must be used. Different procedures might be used to collect data according to the nature of our study.

(3) The analysis and interpretation of the data collected will provide an answer to the question or hypothesis of the study. The correct procedure to analyse the data must be used.

In the previous section, the general components of research used to carry out a research project were presented. Now we have to consider the beginning stages of a research project which involves experimental methodology. The initial steps taken in carrying out a research project are very important and vital for the success of the project itself. A logical progression in starting a research project and setting a careful plan is now provided.

Step 1: Developing a question and/or hypothesis (see Box 6.4 and Box 6.5)

The first step is to formulate a question or a hypothesis. Questions might arise from everyday experience as a teacher (behaviour observation), curiosity from something observed in the classroom, reading other research findings (theories in SLA or/and empirical studies) as a source for more questioning. All these sources might provide the stimulus for formulating a research question. Let us pretend that we want to investigate the role of grammar instruction in second language learning, and we formulate the following question: would grammar instruction have a positive effect on second language learning?

This question is really too broad and the next step is to break down the question and narrow the scope of the research. Therefore, a more focused question will be: would a comprehension-based type of grammar instruction have a positive effect on Japanese second language learning? In order to focus even more on the scope of our research we should identify the type of grammar instruction we want to investigate, the context and the population involved in our study. As a result of these processes a more focused question will be: would processing instruction have a positive effect on the acquisition of Japanese verbal morphology among adult intermediate students of Italian?

As highlighted by Seliger and Shohamy (1989:51), importance and feasibility are the two main components in a research project. Once a general question is formulated, it is necessary to establish whether it is possible to carry out research on such a question. In other words the question to be asked is now: is the general question important and feasible? The importance of a question can be easily demonstrated by a literature review, but the feasibility of a research project might be a more difficult task. These are some of the questions which should be addressed at the initial stage of research to avoid having to abandon a study at a later stage due to unforeseen problems. Once we have generated a question, there are several possibilities in terms of settings (natural or classroom) and type of approach (synthetic or analytic, see Seliger and Shohamy 1989:25, for more details). The synthetic approach would view the research as a combination of factors to be analysed (classroom practice as an exercise made up of different parts: drill, group, pairs, etc.). To isolate one form from another may distort its role. Using this approach may allow us to evaluate the relative contribution each form of practice makes to the overall process of acquisition. The analytic approach looks at some aspects in isolation and requires a clear definition of the terms which will become the focus of research (a specific construct to be investigated). It is necessary to acquire the general knowledge and eventually the very specific familiarity with the subject to be investigated. This will be achieved through a contextual process in the development of a research project. This involves the selection of a research problem, and the creation of a rationale for the study through existing knowledge in the literature. Some of the questions which should be asked are:

(a) Are the terms and concepts used in the formulation of the general questions clearly defined? In order to avoid problems of ambiguity and inconsistency the main terms of the research project should be clearly defined.
(b) What logistical and practical problems can be anticipated? Any possible practical obstacle should be looked at in order to anticipate any possible problems arising from the study.

Research starts with a preconceived notion, a sort of prediction or hypothesis to be confirmed or rejected. This design is hypothesis driven and the hypothesis is usually grounded in a theory which attempts to explain the behaviour in question. A so-called deductive purpose aims at demonstrating the existence of a clear relationship between variables or factors which are taught and some aspects of language acquisition.

Box 6.4   Generating research questions: summary

Step 1. Make explicit the precise area of an investigation.
Step 2. Identify specific aspects of particular interest, within the area of general concern.
Step 3. Critically analyze the relevant literature review to identify a gap in the knowledge.
Step 4. Formulate a hypothesis or research question.

Box 6.5   Hypothesis: definition

A tentative proposition which is subject to verification through subsequent investigation. In many cases hypotheses are hunches that the researcher has about the existence of relationship between variables.

Step 2: Writing the research plan/project

A careful plan needs to be developed. This implies the process of organizing the elements or components of a research study. The lack of a coherent plan might have a devastating effect on the clarity of the project and the impossibility of finding answers to the questions posed. As stated earlier, research is a scientific, methodical and disciplined inquiry. It is structured, organized and systematic. In designing a research project once the research question has been focused, a clear plan is needed. A coherent plan should clarify the focus of the researcher and define the goals and questions of the experimental research. One of the main tasks to be addressed is the identification of the main variables involved in a study: the independent (the predictor) and the dependent (the predicted) variables. The predictor will predict what will happen to another variable to which it is related in some way. The so-called independent variable is the factor manipulated by the researcher, and the dependent is the means by which any changes are measured.

Once we have reached a clear definition of the variables (see Box 6.6) and the terms in the main question, the next step is formulating the research hypotheses which will be confirmed or rejected after the data analysis process. Although we might believe that only one factor or variable is responsible for the effects measured, we have to consider other variables which have to be controlled. This is to ensure that our research has a sound design and that a careful methodology is used in the investigation. Our main goal is to make the research more effective in order to strengthen the reliability of the data. Let us suppose that we want to investigate the effect of a teaching technique on the acquisition of a specific linguistic feature of a target foreign language. We predict that this technique is better than another and we embark in a classroom-based experiment evaluating the effects of the two techniques on the acquisition of the targeted feature. Despite the fact that we might find that there is a relationship between a particular teaching technique (independent variable) and scores on various tests (dependent variable), it would be still necessary to consider other factors interfering with the results (e.g. subject variables: sex roles, age, reaction to testing, distribution of males/females and external variables: teachers, method of teaching, effect of time, attrition of subjects, etc.). It is possible that other variables influence our findings. We will come back later on the two concepts of validity and reliability of experimental study.

Box 6.6   Fundamentals for starting research

- Clarify what aspects of a general area are of most concern to you.
- Think about the purpose of the research.
- Why am I interested in finding out more about the issue? This helps to identify a list of priorities and then to decide what is the most important.

The research cycle

Research as defined by Seliger and Shohamy (1989:2) is cyclical. Experimental research is a cyclical process which involves interrelated phases. When we first approach research, we develop an interest and a purpose which is transferred into the formulation of a question or hypothesis. We then review the literature and, as a result of placing the research problem within a larger body of knowledge, we design and plan the research according to the specific problem we want to investigate. We then select a collection procedure for gathering the necessary data and eventually obtain the results which will be analysed. In the last phase of the research process we interpret and summarize the results. The interpretation of the findings will lead us back to the starting point (question or hypothesis). The answers we have obtained, however, do not close the research cycle as other questions arise and our conclusions lead to other questions as you can see from the student's statement at the beginning of the chapter. The following are the main phases taken in the research cycle:

(A) From the general to a more focused research problem – formulate questions/hypotheses

This process involves the identification of a research area, aims and objectives and the formulation of questions and hypotheses for which the research project is justified. As previously indicated it will involve the researcher to identify a general research area, narrow down the topic and formulate some researchable questions or hypothesis.

(B) Design the study

This process involves the selection of subjects, materials and overall methodological procedure. In the following paragraph, we will describe some of the experimental designs.

(C) Collect the data

This process involves making the decision on what constitutes data and the type of data suitable for the research question to be investigated. Once a specific design for the research project has been selected, consistent with the aims of the study, decision has to be taken on which procedure needs to be used to collect the data. What constitutes data needs to be established and the procedures to collect the data need to be chosen. The variables which need to be investigated in a given research study need to be identified and defined. Determining what constitutes data in second language research depends on the focus of the study and the specific variables which have been identified. You need to operationalize the variables in your study, i.e. you have to identify specific behaviours which would provide evidence to describe the variables involved in your study. Once you have decided on the data to collect, the next step is to decide how to collect them. The data collected through the assessment of a specific behaviour in the experimental method occur in a number of forms: observation schemes, questionnaires, tests.

Observation schemes

Observation as a research tool in an experimental study is perhaps one of the oldest methods used to collect data in the classroom. The rationale behind the growth of classroom observation as a means for experimental methodology is to provide detailed and precise information about what goes on in the classroom for various purposes. Although, it was always considered a major way of collecting qualitative data, in recent years we have witnessed a shift in the use of observation schemes towards more deductive, quantitative and experimental study. This is the case of an observation scheme called COLT (Communicative Orientation of Language Teaching, see Spada, 1990). COLT was developed in a research project investigating differences in instructional treatments. More specifically this observation scheme identified the main characteristics of communicative language teaching and was a very sensitive instrument in the communicative orientation of second language teaching. COLT has two parts: part A was developed to describe classroom events at the level of classroom tasks and activities, while part B analyses the communicative features of verbal interactions between instructors and students in classroom activities. This observation scheme includes five major categories (Spada, 1990):

activity type (type of tasks learners are required to do)
participant organization (type of interaction)
content (type of instruction, meaning-based or form-based in its orientation)
student modality (time spent on developing the four skills)
materials (type, length and source of materials used).

Each of these categories is divided into subcategories (Spada, 1987, 1990) designed to describe categories of classroom procedures based on theories of second language acquisition and teaching. COLT describes differences in the kind of instruction students receive in the language classroom. The classroom is observed by an investigator and all the activities are coded and subsequently analysed. In order to establish differences among groups in the categories considered, the analysis involves the calculation of the amount of time spent by teachers and students on the various categories and subcategories of the observation scheme. By following these procedures we obtain percentages for the various categories.

Let's assume that we are carrying out an experiment to establish possible instructional differences among three groups learning Japanese at intermediate level through a communicative programme. The data are collected by an observer using COLT part A in three classrooms for 4 weeks. The results of the analysis indicate that the three classes are similar in most features. For example, in the case of the participant organization category, the analysis shows that instruction is teacher-centred for 50 percent of the time for all classes. Similarly, in terms of the student modality category, the three classes spend most of their time primarily listening to the teacher or other students (45 percent of the time). However, some of the results of this analysis show some important instructional differences among the three groups. In the case of the content category, although the three classes spent most of the time (50%) focusing exclusively on meaning-based activities and less time on form-based activities, the analysis shows that there are some individual group differences in the amount of time spent on form-based instruction (group one 32 percent, group two 22 percent, group three 9 percent).

Questionnaires

In experimental methodology, questionnaires are often used to collect data on phenomena not easily observed such as attitudes or motivation. They are also used for two further reasons, i.e. to collect data on the processes involved in using languages and to obtain background information. Questionnaires (see Figure 6.1) could provide, among other features, the following:

(a) background information
(b) quality and quantity of the learner's previous exposure to different types of foreign language learning
(c) learners attitudes to the different language-teaching methods already experienced
(d) learner's expectations, attitudes and degree of motivation to learn a language

We also require L2 learners involved in an experiment to fill a consent form (see Figure 6.2).

PROFILE QUESTIONNAIRE

1) Name: 2) Nationality:
3) Mother Tongue: 4) Age:
5) Sex: 6) Degree course:
7) Previous study or knowledge of Italian: yes   no
                                                 ☐   ☐
if yes what kind?

Other foreign languages you know or you are studying:
French   ☐
German   ☐
Spanish   ☐
Greek   ☐
others(specify)   ☐
Do you have any qualification in a foreign language? If yes what mark did you get?
O level ☐   specify the mark you obtained _____
A level ☐   specify the mark you obtained _____

8)   yes   no
   a) Do you use Italian in any way with someone outside the classroom? ☐   ☐
   b) do you have any contact with native speakers outside the classroom ☐   ☐
   c) have you ever visited Italy   ☐   ☐
       if yes for how long?

Figure 6.1 Profile questionnaire.

CONSENT FORM

This is a consent form for you to take part to an experiment in language instruction. You will be tested and with other students receive instruction and practice on a particular structure in Italian. Your answers will remain confidential. All the results will be reported through statistical representations and no individual results will be made available.

Your participation is only voluntary and you may choose to leave at anytime and not complete the experiment. If you agree to participate, please indicate by signing below.

I agree to participate in this experiment. My participation is voluntary and I have read the above informed consent information.

Name

L1

Signature   Date

Figure 6.2 Consent form.

Tests

Tests are a procedure used to collect data about the subjects' knowledge of a second language in areas such as vocabulary, grammar, reading, metalinguistic awareness and general proficiency. There are different types of language tests (see Bacham and Palmer, 1996) such as achievement test, proficiency test and diagnosis test.

In experimental study, we use achievement tests (dependent variable) to measure the effects of the independent variable (e.g. method, technique or an instructional approach to teaching). In the example below, two tests (interpretation and production tasks) were developed for an experimental study investigating the effects of different instructional treatments in the acquisition of Japanese (Lee and Benati, 2007a) present forms. The interpretation test constructed consisted of 20 sentences (five affirmative, five negative and 10 distracters in a different tense). Participants had to rely on the verb (in final position) to establish whether the sentence was in the present negative or affirmative forms. If they were not sure they could choose the 'not sure' (*warikasen*) option. The scoring was calculated as follows: incorrect response = 0 point, correct response = 1 point.

Test 1

Interpretation task

Listen to the following sentences and establish whether the sentence in the present form is negative or affirmative or you are not sure.

1	☐ Koutei	☐ Hitei	☐ Wakarimasen
2	☐ Koutei	☐ Hitei	☐ Wakarimasen
3	☐ Koutei	☐ Hitei	☐ Wakarimasen
4	☐ Koutei	☐ Hitei	☐ Wakarimasen
5	☐ Koutei	☐ Hitei	☐ Wakarimasen
6	☐ Koutei	☐ Hitei	☐ Wakarimasen
7	☐ Koutei	☐ Hitei	☐ Wakarimasen
8	☐ Koutei	☐ Hitei	☐ Wakarimasen
9	☐ Koutei	☐ Hitei	☐ Wakarimasen
10	☐ Koutei	☐ Hitei	☐ Wakarimasen
11	☐ Koutei	☐ Hitei	☐ Wakarimasen

12	☐ Koutei	☐ Hitei	☐ Wakarimasen
13	☐ Koutei	☐ Hitei	☐ Wakarimasen
14	☐ Koutei	☐ Hitei	☐ Wakarimasen
15	☐ Koutei	☐ Hitei	☐ Wakarimasen
16	☐ Koutei	☐ Hitei	☐ Wakarimasen
17	☐ Koutei	☐ Hitei	☐ Wakarimasen
18	☐ Koutei	☐ Hitei	☐ Wakarimasen
19	☐ Koutei	☐ Hitei	☐ Wakarimasen
20	☐ Koutei	☐ Hitei	☐ Wakarimasen

Sentences heard by learners:

1. *Watashi wa tomodachi to dekakemasu*
2. *Watashi wa tomodachi to dekakemasen*
3. *no shumatsu tomodachi to sugoshimashita*
4. *Watashi wa terebi o mimasen*
5. *totemo ii hon o yomishamita*
6. *Joan to gekijyou ni ikimashita*
7. *wa terebi o mimasu*
8. *ronbun o kakimashita*
9. *nohongo de shinbun o yomimasen*
10. *uchi/ie ni kaerimashita*
11. *san-ji ni basu ni norimasen*
12. *uchi/ie ni kaerimashita*
13. *watashi wa Alessandro to hanashimasu*
14. *Bernie to hanashimashita*
15. *watashi wa gimu ni ikimasen*
16. *watashi wa gimu ni ikimashita*
17. *watashi wa gekijyou ni ikimasu*
18. *Kinou watashi wa john to kouen a arukimashita*
19. *gengogaku o benkyou shimasu*
20. *bar de wain o takusan*

A sentence-completion production task to measures the learner's ability to produce correct forms. In the case of the positive vs. negative present forms, the written production grammar test consisted of ten sentences to complete (five affirmative and five negative) in the present form. The scoring procedure was the following: a fully correct form received 1 point and no points to a form that was not fully correct.

Test 2

Complete the following sentences using the present form.

1. Watashi wa Italia ni --------------(vado).
2. Watashi wa Italia ni--------------(non vado).
3. Watashi wa mainichi tenisu o --------------(gioco).
4. Watashi wa mainichi tenisu o --------------(non gioco).
5. Watashi wa maiban tereibi o--------------(non guardo).
6. Watashi wa denwa de Paul to--------------(parlo).
7. Watashi wa denwa de Paul to --------------(non parlo).
8. Watashi wa mainichi osoku made--------------(dormo).
9. Watashi wa rajio o--------------(ascolto).
10. Watashi wa rajio o --------------(non ascolto).

(D) Analyse the data

This process involves making decisions on the type of analysis required. In experimental data analysis, different designs imply different methods of analysis. Let us suppose that an experiment has been carried out to compare the performance of two groups of subjects – an experimental group and a control group. An independent *t-test* is a method used to compare the means of two groups and helps to determine that the statistical difference between two groups is not due to chance. The result of this test provides the researcher with a t-value which is entered in a table which indicates whether the *t*-value is statistically significant. In order to provide a better picture when presenting the result of a *t*-test it is advisable to carry out descriptive analysis and display the mean (X), standard deviation (SD) and size of sample (N).

The group mean is the average of the scores in each instructional group. The standard deviation provides information on the range of scores obtained by each group. In Table 6.1 an example of a table used in summarizing descriptive analysis in an experimental study is provided. In Table 6.1 the mean and standard deviation of three groups in three different tests are summarized.

One-way ANOVA is the method used to examine the differences in more than two groups, for example, two experimental groups and one control group. The One-way ANOVA procedure produces a one-way analysis of variance for a quantitative dependent variable by a single factor (independent) variable. The analysis will result in an F-value which is entered in a table to establish

Table 6.1 Means and Standard Deviations (pre-test, post-test 1, post-test 2)

Variable	Treatments	Mean (X)	SD	N
pre-test				
GROUP	1 input	3.8462	1.4051	13
GROUP	2 output	4.0769	1.1152	13
GROUP	3 control	3.7692	1.0127	13
post-test 1				
GROUP	1 input	8.3846	.9608	13
GROUP	2 output	5.8462	.9871	13
GROUP	3 control	4.0000	.8165	13
post-test 2				
GROUP	1 input	8.1538	1.0682	13
GROUP	2 output	5.6923	.9473	13
GROUP	3 control	3.3846	.9608	13

whether the F-value is significant. When the F-value is significant, the researcher will reject the null hypothesis of no difference and, therefore, establish the existence of some differences in the groups. Let us suppose that we want to investigate the effects of two different grammar treatments and two instructional groups and a control group are set. In this case, the independent variable is the three conditions representing the treatments and the dependent is the scores of tests developed to measure the effects of those instructional conditions. Although we have discovered that the means of the three groups are different, we need to carry out an ANOVA to verify tests whether there is significance (significance of the F-value) somewhere among the means of the three groups. The ANOVA in Table 6.2 shows whether there is significance in the following variables: treatment, time and interaction between treatment and time. In this case (Table 6.2) the results of the ANOVA shows that there is statistical difference for treatment, (F-value inferior to 0.05) and for time (F-value inferior to 0.05), but not for the interaction between treatment and time (F-value superior to 0.05).

However, in addition to determining that differences exist among the means, you may want to know which means differ. Post-hoc range tests (e.g. Tukey honestly significant difference test, Scheffe test) can determine which means differ. Range tests identify homogeneous subsets of means that are not different from each other and yield a matrix where asterisks indicate significantly different group means at an alpha level of 0.05 (significance numerical

Table 6.2 ANOVA (Repeated Measures) summary table (post-tests)

Source of Variation	SS	DF	MS	F(value)	Significance
TREATMENT	273.10	2	136.55	85.09	.000
TIME	2.17	2	2.17	9.14	.005
TREATMENT X					
TIME	.79	2	.40	1.68	.201

measure as in the case of the ANOVA). Most of the analysis techniques used in applied linguistics can be carried out with a computer and a number of statistical packages have been designed and are available.

(E) Interpret and discuss the findings and draw some conclusions

This process involves the interpretation of the results in the light of the research questions/hypotheses raised. Our intention is not only to report and summarize research results but also to identify the implications of the results and recommend possible further research.

It is now time to summarize the results reporting the main findings. The final three steps are: reporting, summarizing and interpreting the results. In the reporting and summarizing phases, you have to report the results obtained in your study through the analysis techniques you have used. You are allowed to use tables, charts, category lists or graphs to present your data in a clear way. An important element is the inclusion of the reliability and validity of the procedures you used to collect data so that the research is replicable. In the interpreting phase, you go beyond the results obtained in your analysis and discuss the implications in relation to more general theoretical and practical issues of the research topic. You discuss the meaning of the research results and place them in a broader and general context. You also recommend different applications for your study and possible new areas of research which derive from your research. It is important that the discussion, reflections and recommendations you make are linked to the context in which the research was conducted. Research is a cyclical exercise formed by a sequence of events (see Figure 6.1) which leads us back to the starting point in order to answer our questions. However, in the nature of research the more answers we obtain, the more questions arise and lead us to more problems, more questions and more research areas.

The project

The Research Project provides an opportunity for the researcher to undertake a study in depth, extend an understanding of the theoretical and practical basis of a specific area and topic, demonstrate the ability to reflect and conduct a study on a specific area, and demonstrate awareness of potential and limitations of the research methods chosen.

CHAPTER 1: INTRODUCTION
Significance of the Study
Definition of Terms
Outline of the Thesis

CHAPTER 2: BACKGROUND AND MOTIVATION FOR THE STUDY
Review of the literature
Motivation and justification of the study
Hypotheses and/or Research Questions

CHAPTER 3: METHOD AND PROCEDURE
Overview of the Study
Participants
Materials
Procedure
Scoring and Analyses

CHAPTER 4: RESULTS
Overview of the Results
Statistics
Summary of the Results

CHAPTER 5: DISCUSSION AND CONCLUSION
Discussion
Limitations of the Study
Implications
Future Research
Conclusion

REFERENCES

APPENDICES

Figure 6.3 The research project structure.

In a research project (see Figure 6.3), the researcher should introduce and describe the problem first. This is the introduction section (Chapter 1) where the researcher discusses the purpose of the study, the significance of the problem and the questions to be addressed. The researcher would need to give reasons as to why the topic is of sufficient importance for it to be researched.

The literature review (Chapter 2) is a report on the theory and research evidence relevant to the problem (focusing on different aspects of the problem). In the literature review, we provide a conceptual and theoretical context in which the topic for research can be situated. In the description of the literature, the researcher focuses on the theoretical claims made in the research. A survey of findings is made, particularly the major findings of the relevant studies, with a discussion of how they were obtained and what can be learned from them, particularly in relation to the specific research we want to conduct. An important part of the literature review (see Box 6.7) is the critique of the research studies, pointing out problems in design, argumentation, analysis and conclusions.

Box 6.7 Why we write a literature review

- To give reasons why the topic is of sufficient importance for it to be researched.
- To provide the reader with a brief up-to-date account and discussion of literature on the issues relevant to the topic.
- To provide a conceptual and theoretical context in which the topic for research can be positioned.
- To discuss relevant research carried out on the same topic or similar topics.

At the end of the literature review, the researcher will formulate the main hypothesis or question of the project. A hypothesis is a tentative proposition which is subject to verification through subsequent investigation. In many cases hypotheses are hunches that the researcher has about the existence of relationship between variables. In questions, the researcher makes explicit the precise area of an investigation, identify specific aspects of particular interest, within the area of general concern.

The purpose of the literature review is to provide a theoretical framework for the study we want to conduct and a description of how different studies could contribute to the topic. This would lead to a statement and a rationale for the study.

In the Design and methodology (Chapter 3) part of the project, the researcher would need to provide a clear description of the research questions or hypotheses and of the different variables of the study. The design would need to be presented in detail, so that the reader has a very clear idea of the method used by the researcher to investigate the research problem (questions/hypotheses). Common components of this section are: description of the participants involved in the project (population), procedures used to collect data (e.g. materials, tests), procedures to analyse data (statistical analysis).

In the data analysis chapter (Chapter 4), the researcher reports on the results of data collected and the analysis conducted in the study. In the final part of the project, the researcher provides a summary statement of the research results obtained and then a discussion of their meaning in relation to previous literature and in a broader context and perspective. This includes the contribution of the results to the general area of research, their implications and whether they can lead to recommendations, limitations of the present study and suggestions for further research.

The reference list contains the sources and references used and consulted, and the appendices includes additional material used, tests, raw data, questionnaires or any other procedures used which is to detailed to be included in the body of the research report.

Designs in experimental studies

Experimental methodology has been evaluated over the years, however, many scholars such as Long (1984), are committed to experimentation as the strongest research design available for foreign and second language programme evaluation. The way to strengthen the internal validity of classroom experimentation is to monitor classroom processes in experimental and control conditions. This monitoring has different purposes such as checking the feasibility and degree of implementation of classroom procedures promoted by the programme or monitoring the interactions between old and new procedures. Long (1984:419), however, reserves the term 'process' for a main purpose 'monitoring for the maintenance of key planned differences between treatments'. This is also the point of view of Spada (1990) who claims that 'a process component in the experimental methodology will provide support and explanations for the findings of product evaluations'. Having established the need for a product and process approach to experimental design, we should move to a description of experimental research in order to explain the components of the experimental method and the way this methodology can be implemented by a researcher. Experimental research is carried out to explore the strength of a relationship between variables. As practitioners, we often want to investigate the relationship between a variable such as a teaching approach and a second variable represented by the test scores on an achievement test. The teaching approach will be given the label of independent variable as we expect that this variable would influence the other variable (the test). The variable upon which the independent variable is acting is called the dependent variable.

The independent variables in this study are obviously the two instructional treatments and the dependent variables are the three tasks used to measure the possible effects of the two different treatments. Experimental research is carefully planned and constructed so that the variables involved in the study are controlled and manipulated. In the study mentioned above, we can identify the three main components of an experimental research design (see Seliger and Shohamy, 1989:136):

(a) the subject pool;
(b) the instructional treatment (independent factor);
(c) the measurement of the instructional treatment (dependent factor).

(a) The main objective of experimental design broadly speaking is to measure the relative effects of different instructional treatments given to subjects arranged in groups. Groups can be formed by the researcher specifically for an experiment (Quasi-experimental designs) or pre-existing groups can be used. In the latter case, we talk about true experimental designs. In forming experimental groups, the researcher needs to take into account subject variables and uses randomization or matching procedures to make sure that the groups belong to the same population.

(b) The instructional treatment is the independent variable in an experimental research design and it is specifically constructed for the experiment. An instructional treatment refers to a technique, method or material presented under controlled circumstances which we want to apply to groups in order to measure its effects.

(c) The measurement is the way in which the effects of the treatment are evaluated and observed. Different types of test are the logical way to evaluate the effectiveness of a treatment.

As previously stated, normally in experimental classroom-based studies, the independent variable is a stimulus (e.g. a new method, technique) and the dependent variable is a response to that stimulus (e.g. student's performance on a test). Experiments in classroom settings are usually quasi-experimental and rarely experimental. The main difference between these two designs is that in a quasi-experimental design the researcher undertakes his research with groups that have been constituted by means and not by random procedure as in the case of a 'true' experimental design. The distinction will be clearer when we identify and explain the essential features of the pre-experimental, quasi-experimental and 'true' experimental designs. However, before we do that, we need to use some specific symbols to describe the main element of experimental research. Campbell and Stanley (1963) have used specific symbols to refer to the main components of the experimental methodology:

X = represents the exposition of a group to a kind of treatment, and the effects of which
     we intend to measure;
O = refers to the process of measurement or observation of a particular treatment;
R = indicates the use of a random procedure.

The experimental methodology can be categorized through various designs which reflect the different contexts and conditions in which the research is conducted. There are different ways of carrying out an experiment; however, the design has to be constructed so that variables can be controlled and manipulated and at the same time it is methodologically very rigorous. Let us consider a practical example in which the most appropriate way to collect data is through the experimental method. All language teachers have strong views and beliefs about language teaching and learning and the methods or materials they use. Imagine that we have used a new technique to teach a foreign language and have developed very innovative reading and comprehension type materials for intermediate students. We strongly believe that this material is better and more effective than the more traditional materials used normally. Although convinced that this is the case, you need to persuade your colleagues who do not think the same as they are used to the more traditional set of materials. You need, therefore, to collect some sort of evidence which supports your view and you are presented with many choices. You can interview the students and gather their impressions or you can make an ethnographic record of the teaching and learning in the classroom with the help of an external observer. However, the only way to obtain reliable data in this case is using tests to measure the effects of your new set of materials. You must now decide which research design to follow in order to construct a satisfactory study. In the following section we will explore the different experimental research designs available using this practical example and see how differently we might approach our research.

One shot design

The one shot design is used for pilot studies where researchers want to try out treatments or tests before entering a full experimental design. It is a very basic design and involves the use of a single treatment and a single group (X, O). We may be tempted to use the group of students you are teaching and to test them at the end of the instructional period.

Let's say for example that we develop some new task for teaching Japanese verbal morphology and we want to test their effectiveness. We develop the materials and administer it to a single group. At the end of this experiment, we might find that the students have responded well to the material we have developed and we might conclude that it is very effective.

The main problem with this type of design is that it does not control other factors that might influence your findings. Another problem with this approach is that we do not have information about the individual characteristics of the group involved in the study before the beginning of the instructional treatment. Our inclination would be to exercise a better control over the group involved in the research.

Pre-experimental design: one group pre-test and post-test design

In this design we intend to use the same group as its own control through a pre-test and post-test procedure in order to eliminate a number of subject variables as only one group is used and the subjects are tested twice on the dependent variable. Let's say that we want to measure the value of a new method or technique in the teaching of Japanese. In the case of our practical example, one group of students will be tested before the treatment begins. Following a week of that treatment, the researcher will administer a post-test to measure the effects of the treatment on students' performance and will proceed to account for differences between pre- and post-test by reference to the effects of the instructional treatment. Let's suppose that the researcher has found out that post-test scores indicate an improvement in learners' performance compared with the pre-test scores. How justified are we in attributing the cause of these differences between pre- and post-test to the experimental treatment? Initially, we might argue that there is a casual relationship between treatment and the measurement of the treatment; however things are rather more complex and we can't simply make an assumption. The main problem using this design is that we cannot be sure that the possible positive results and changes between the pre-test applied before the treatment and the post-test carried out after the treatment are due to the delivery of that treatment. Factors other than our treatment could be responsible for these changes. We can't be confident that the observed changes in learners' performance are to be attributed to our treatment because in the confines of our classroom we have not excluded or controlled all other extraneous variables. The previous exposure to other material inside and outside the classroom, the teacher, the classroom organization, the individual characteristics of the population and many other factors (e.g. the use of the pre-test might have sensitized the group towards specific aspects of the treatment) might all or individually have affected and influenced student's improved performance. These variables outside the experiment are a threat to the validity of the experiment and a different design will have to be considered to address this problem.

The 'true' experimental design

In an experimental design (see Box 6.8), the independent variable is manipulated in some ways and its effects measured through some dependent variables while all the other factors are controlled. In the so-called 'true' experimental design, the treatment is administered to one group and the group's performance is compared with another group which has not received the same treatment. The difference between this design and the one described previously (the pre-experimental design) is that the 'true' experimental design involves the use of two groups which have been formed through a process of randomization.

Randomization would ensure that subjects are equally distributed to groups and by doing that it is assumed that all the independent variables are controlled. It is also the addition of a control group in our experimental design that increases the soundness of our experimental methodology. If both groups are made equivalent before the beginning of the instructional period then any other possible extraneous variable might be present in both groups. Many of the possible internal validity threats are controlled in the pre- and post-test control group design. One of the possible internal validity factors called task sensitivity can be controlled by adding two more groups that have not experienced the pre-test measures.

A true experimental design was used in a classroom study (Lee and Benati, 2007a) were the possible effects of two different instructional interventions (structured input practice vs. traditional instruction) in the acquisition of Japanese use of affirmative vs. negative present forms were investigated. The relative effects of an innovative approach to grammar instruction were compared with a traditional approach to grammar instruction Learners consisted of twenty-seven Italian native-speakers (beginner students) who were learning Japanese in a private school in Italy. They were randomly assigned to two groups. One group received the innovative instructional treatment and the other group the traditional instructional treatment. A pre- and post-test procedure was adopted. Two tests were developed for each linguistic feature and consisted of an aural interpretation task and a written completion production task at sentence level. The pre-tests were used to measure learner's performance before the beginning of the instructional treatments. After the treatments which lasted over two days, learners received a battery of post-tests (interpretation and production tests). The scores were measured with the use of a statistical analysis procedure which revealed that subjects in the innovative groups performed better than subjects in the traditional group in the interpretation measure and the two groups performed equally in the production test. The results were proved to be parallel to those obtained by other studies investigating other languages and grammatical features.

Question to reflect on . . .

Can you select one experimental study in Japanese and identify the following:

1 Research Question/motivation of the study
2 Subjects
3 Method
4 Type of data
5 Type of analysis
6 Main findings

The quasi-experimental-design

This design is also called quasi-experimental and is very economical as it allows us to use existing groups rather than reassign subjects to groups. The problem with this design is that we are not sure whether the two groups are equivalent before the treatment. One way to avoid this is to match the subjects in the two groups according to various characteristics (sex, aptitude, language, scores, etc.). This would increase the comparability of the groups. However, researchers use randomization to reduce the bias factor in assigning subjects to groups and controlling extraneous variables as they are equally distributed by chance between the groups. This procedure also provides an option for not using the pre-test procedure.

A quasi experimental design was used in a study comparing the teaching of Japanese in the ALM and the Counseling-Learning Approach (Samimy, 1989). The main aim of this study was to measure whether Counseling-Learning Approach would be an effective language teaching methods in improving learners' communicative and linguistics competence. The study involved 29 participants, all studying Japanese in an undergraduate programme at the University of Illinois Urbana-Champaign. At the beginning of the semester, questionnaires were used to gather information about student's background, motivation, attitude, anxiety and self-esteem. The two control groups received a modified version of the ALM. The experimental group was taught using the Counseling-Learning Approach. Communicative Competence Tests were used to measure learners' performance. The statistical analysis revealed that there was no statistical difference between the experimental and the control groups on communicative competence measures. However, the descriptive analysis showed that experimental group scores were higher than the control groups scores in the communicative tests.

Box 6.8   Experimental study: main characteristics

The Participant
The treatment (independent factor)
The measurement (dependent factor)

Internal and external validity

The main purpose of research methodology is to make the research design as effective and valid as possible. The main goal is to make sure that the results of the study we have conducted are valid internally and externally. What does this mean? Internal invalidity of findings occurs when the findings might have been affected by other factors (see Seliger and Shohamy, 1989 for a full discussion of external and internal validity factors). External invalidity is when the results cannot be extended or applied to outside contexts. One of the main internal factors that might invalidate findings is for instance the size and characteristics of participants in an experimental study. The characteristics of the subjects and the number of students involved are two important factors we need to take into consideration when we embark in a classroom study. Sometimes we assume that the population involved in a research project is representative of the general population to which the research applies. However, subjects in a group are affected by many variables (e.g. attitude, motivation, gender, age). The question we need to address before we start collecting our data is: are the groups representative samples of the same population? In order to equally distribute subject variables to groups, a random procedure might be used so that we can claim that the subject variables are divided by random chance. Alternatively, a matching procedure can be used to match subjects to groups in terms of the factors we believe that might have an impact on the results of the study.

The size of subject population could also be a factor influencing the validity and reliability of the results. Small populations magnify the effects of individual variability, the greater the size, the smaller the effect of individual variability.

The calculation of the time needed for data collection or the experiment treatment is also another factor for internal validity which should be looked at in a classroom study. How can I establish how much time is needed to show an effect for a treatment? There is no hard and fast rule for deciding when enough time has been given to collecting a valid sample of data; it is relative to factors such as context, amount of available time, sensitivity of the instruments used to elicit data, etc.

The instruments used to collect data could also influence internal validity. Sometimes instruments (task sensitivity) are used as a tool to obtain information about the status of the subject (pre-test used before the experiment). However, the pre-test could affect the internal validity of the experiment as learners can become test-wise and this practice might affect the subjects' performance. In order to make a study internally valid we need to be able to demonstrate that the relationship between the independent and dependent variables is unambiguous and not explained by other variables.

External validity is concerned with applying and generalizing the findings to situations outside those in which the research was conducted. One of the main factors affecting external validity is again the characteristics of the population. The question needed to be addressed is: can we apply the findings obtained in a study to a different population? Can the effects of an instructional treatment on school-age learners be generalized to adults?

The interaction of subject selection and research is another external factor that might influence the findings of a classroom-based study. Very often volunteers have to be used to collect data. The question which needs to be addressed is: to what degree do paid or volunteer subjects represent the general population to which the research will be generalized? It could be said for instance that volunteers might have a better attitude towards an experiment than existing subjects participating in an experiment.

The descriptive explicitness of the independent variable is also a very important factor to be controlled by the researcher. It is crucial to be able to describe the instructional treatment (independent variable) as explicitly as possible providing details of how the treatment is implemented. Linked to this latter factor are the possible effects of the research environment. Learners' awareness of taking part in an experiment might affect the behaviour of the sample the researcher or experimenter effects: the researcher could have a biased attitude for one method or another.

Question to reflect on . . .

Can you select one classroom-based study in Japanese and discuss validity and reliability of the study?

Action research

Action research is a very effective methodology to investigate a problem that needs to be resolved or when some changes are necessary to improve learner's performance. It is usually a method that can be used by individual teacher or a group of teachers working in co-operation.

Teachers are interested in understanding how learning takes place and therefore undertake small-scale studies on their own. Action research can be used in a variety of areas and more specifically in second language research teachers might want to explore and measure the effectiveness of a teaching method in the attempt to find a new replacement and make changes.

Action research is often motivated by teachers reflecting on their current teaching and subsequently identifying a 'problem' related to their teaching.

Ellis (1997:200) has identified three main sources used by teachers to develop an initial research question:

from a theory and previously published research;
from the need of a replication of previous research;
from the need to carry out micro-evaluations of courses, programs or materials.

Teachers must be up-to-date with SLA theory and research findings. Not only because this awareness might help teachers to improve their teaching methodology but also because it could provide the stimulus and motivation to carry outtheir own research to test and measure the effects of a particular SLA theory on language pedagogy. Teachers have the opportunities to replicate a study to measure whether or not previous research findings on the effects of particular methods in language teaching on language learning can be generalized. Teachers can carry out a micro-evaluation of teaching materials, tasks or a particular methodology of approach to language teaching. As Argued by Nunan (1989), this type of action research contains the same components as the experimental method and consists of various stages:

identifying an issue;
describing the issue;
planning the research;
collecting the information;
analysing the information;
drawing a conclusion and making recommendations;
writing a report and disseminating results.

At the beginning a practitioner identifies an issue or a problem related to their own teaching they want to investigate. Let's assume that the problem the teacher has identified is that students do not seem to master some of the morphological and syntactic grammatical features of Japanese he is teaching them. The practitioner decides first of all to evaluate his current teaching method and collects some data through observation and discussion with the students. As a result of the analysis of the data he has collected, he develops the idea that it is his own approach to grammar teaching that causes learners the problem of not mastering the some of the grammatical features of Japanese. As a result of this observation, he makes some recommendations and he suggests that a different approach to grammar teaching would help students to learn the grammatical features of the target language better. He produces some new material to teach the students Japanese and notices that students are performing much better than before. He then decides to disseminate his findings and investigates alternative approaches to grammar teaching.

As previously stated, this approach to classroom research could be very effective in addressing a problem or issues in learning and teaching and provides a possible solution. This method of research is initiated by a problem the practitioner has noticed, therefore a hypothesis is formulated and a form of intervention is devised. An evaluation of possible interventions is carried out and the practitioner plans to disseminate the results of his action research as he is prepared to look at different form of interventions in order to improve his teaching and student's experience.

Despite the importance for teachers to address practical issues in the language classroom and collect their own data, this approach might not be the best approach for conducting research. In fact, there are some methodological faults that the reader needs to be aware of. We cannot establish that students' performance is in any way related to the administration of the new material (treatment) as it could be argued that it was caused by other variables we did not control (e.g. previous knowledge). In the absence of a pre-test we also do not have any measurement of student's knowledge before the beginning of the instructional treatment. We do not have a control group, and therefore we cannot measure the effects of the instructional treatment vs. no treatment. In addition to that, we cannot say whether the performance is due to a particular component of the treatment (explicit information or a particular task) as we do not have a specific and detailed description of the treatment used. Although, action research is a useful tool for teachers to respond actively to everyday classroom problems, this approach has clearly some methodological limitations.

Question to reflect on . . .

Can you select one action research study in Japanese and identify the following:

1 Research question/motivation of the study
2 Subjects
3 Method
4 Type of data
5 Type of analysis
6 Main findings

Summary

In this chapter, we have provided the reader with an overall view of how research in language learning and teaching is conducted using an experimental methodology. We have looked at the main components in classroom-based research (population, data collection and data analysis) and the main designs used, from one shot design to true experimental design. We have also addressed some of issues related to external and internal validity in an experimental study. Finally, we have indicated that action research is a very useful tool for language teachers to carry out research in their own teaching environment.

There is a clear need for research that examines the acquisition of Japanese as a foreign language as it is an area that has received very little attention outside Japan. Teachers and scholars interested in this area should address research in this area adopting research design and conduct classroom-based research using experimental methodology.

More questions to reflect on . . .

(1) Please complete the following task.

You are asked to prepare a detailed research plan for a project of your choice. You have to include the following:

1. Background of your study:
   a. the area and the specific topic
   b. the title of the study
   c. the problem
   d. the purpose of the study (aims, justification, limitations and delimitations)

2. A statement relating to the literature review to be consulted.

3. The design:
   a. the research questions
   b. the research hypotheses
   c. population of the study
   d. data collection methods
   e. data analysis procedures

4. A statement of how results will be presented

5. A statement of what problems you anticipate and expect in your research and the possible solutions.

In this assignment you should demonstrate the ability to:
- Formulate a research question and hypothesis
- Design a research investigation
- Present, analyze and discuss data from a project of your choice
- Draw conclusions and evaluate your proposal

(2) Choose a couple of experimental studies in Japanese and answer the following questions:
    (a) What method did the experimenter use?
    (b) What data collection and date analysis did the experimenter use?
    (c) What results did the experimenter obtain?

Key terms

Action research: an enquiry conducted by a practitioner which is aimed at solving practical problems.

Experimental study/method: an enquiry for testing questions/hypotheses and establishing the strength of a possible relationship between independent and dependent factors.

Reliability: the question we need to address by evaluating a study is whether an independent researcher carrying out the same study would obtain the same results.

Validity: the question we need to address by evaluating a study is whether what has been measured is what we were supposed to measure. Also the extent to which the findings from one study can be generalized.

Further reading

Mackey, A. and Gass, S. M. (2005). *Second Language Research: Methodology and Design*. Mahwah, NJ: Lawrence Erlbaum Associates.

Nunan, D. (1989). *Understanding Language Classrooms: A Guide for Instructors Initiated Action*. New York: Prentice-Hall.

Sanz, C. (Ed.) (2005). *Mind and Context in Adult Second Language Acquisition*. Washington, DC: Georgetown University Press.

Seliger, H. and Shohany, E. (1989). *Second Language Research Methods*. Oxford: OUP.

A Classroom Experimental Study on the Effects of Processing Instruction in the Acquisition of Japanese

7

Chapter Outline

Introduction

In this chapter, we present the results of a classroom-based experimental study conducted to measure secondary effects for PI. The intent is to show to readers how an experimental study is conducted in the language classroom and describe how the findings are presented, in the hope that it can be a stimulus for teachers to undertake their own research project.

Background and motivation

Introduction

Van Patten (1996) has argued that a type of instructional intervention called PI (see Chapter 4 in this book), which helps learners to process information via comprehension practice, is a more effective type of instruction than that which requires learners to produce language too prematurely. PI is thought to be more effective than traditional instruction (explicit information + output practice) as it provides a more direct route for the learner to convert input to intake. Input processing (see Chapter 1 in this book) is what and how learners initially perceive and process linguistic data in the language they hear or read. As previously discussed in Chapter 1 and 4 of this book, only a portion of the input is initially processed by L2 learners and this is due to processing limitations. This, from a psycholinguistic perspective, is explained by the fact that input does not automatically enter learners' brains during their exposure to it. Learners filter input through internal processors they possess.

Intake refers to the linguistic data in the input that learners attend and hold in working memory during online comprehension. Changing the way learners process input might enrich learner's intake, have an effect on their developing system and subsequently have an impact on how learners produce the L2. The question is how learners initially perceive and process linguistic data in the language they hear or read. According to Van Patten (1996), learners make form–meaning connections from the input they received as they connect particular meanings to particular forms (grammatical or lexical). Research on input processing (Van Patten, 2002, 2003, 2004) attempts to describe what linguistic data learners attend to during comprehension, which ones they do not attend to, what grammatical roles learners assign to nouns and how position in an utterance influences what gets processed.

Van Patten (1996, 2002, 2003, 2004) has identified some strategies (see also Chapter 1 in this book) used by learners to decode input and he has addressed the question of which features learners attend to in the input. The following perceptual strategies are relevant to this study:

P1b learners prefer processing lexical items to grammatical items for semantic information (The Lexical Preference Principle);

P1d learners tend to process items in sentence initial position before those in final position and those in medial position (The Sentence Location Principle).

In Van Patten's view (1996) the main objective of PI is to help learners to circumvent the strategies used by them to derive intake data by making them rely exclusively on form and structure to derive meaning from input. In order to achieve this goal PI must provide learners with a type of comprehension practice called SIA which should force learners to process the target form in the input and to make form–meaning connections. Van Patten (1996, 2000, 2002) has suggested that PI provides a more effective practice than traditional instruction as it equips learners with the tools to convert input into intake. Wong (2004a) has argued that PI 'pushes learners to abandon their inefficient processing strategies for more optimal ones so that better form–meaning connections are made' (p. 35).

The general findings (see also Chapter 4 in this book) of studies measuring the effects of PI (see for a full review Van Patten, 2002; Lee, 2004; Benati and Lee, 2008) vs. traditional output-based instruction (traditional instruction as described by Van Patten and Cadierno, 1993) show that learners receiving PI seem to benefit in their ability to process input (interpretation tasks) as well as being able to access the target feature when performing production tasks. Unlike this type of instruction (paradigmatic explanation of rules in which is followed by output oral and written practice) where the focus of instruction is in the manipulation of the learners' output to effect changes in their developing system, the purpose of PI is to alter how learners process input and to encourage better form–meaning mapping that results in a grammatically richer intake. Therefore, while output-practice may help to develop fluency and accuracy in production it is not responsible for getting the grammar into the learner's head.

Measuring primary effects for PI

Van Patten and Cadierno (1993) have initially investigated whether PI would alter the First Noun Principle (P2). Van Patten and Cadierno (1993) investigated the impact of PI and TI on the acquisition of Spanish direct object pronouns. The results showed that PI is superior to TI and very beneficial for learners. PI improved learners' ability at interpreting object pronouns in Spanish correctly and furthermore the study demonstrated that PI was also effective in improving learners' production, as the positive effects for PI were not only limited to input processing but were also observable in learners' accuracy to produce the target feature. PI was overall superior to TI.

The results of this original study were confirmed by findings of similar studies which investigated the effects of processing instruction on different linguistic features and processing problems. Cadierno (1995) set out to investigate the effects of PI on a different processing problem (Lexical Preference Principle). The linguistic item of Spanish which was researched was the Spanish 'preterite tense'. Benati (2001) conducted an investigation on the effects of two types of PI and TI on the acquisition of a feature of the Italian verbal morphology system (the future tense). The impact of the two instructional treatments (PI vs. TI and a control group) was investigated on the Lexical Preference Principle which has an effect on the linguistic item under investigation. Cheng (2004) measured the effects of PI on the acquisition of copular verbs in Spanish (*ser* and *estar*). One of the processing principles (Preference for Nonredundancy) was particularly relevant for this study as copular verbs in Spanish are of low communicative value for L2 learners and redundant features of Spanish.

Van Patten and Wong (2004) carried out a study comparing the effects of PI and TI on the French *faire* causative. Of relevance to this study was the First Noun Principle.

Other studies have measured the primary effects for PI compared with a different and more meaning output-based type of instruction. Farley (2001a, 2001b, 2004a) compared the effects of PI vs. meaning output-based instruction (MOI) on the acquisition of the Spanish subjunctive. Unlike TI, the MOI contained no mechanical drills and the activities developed for the treatment were based on the tenets of structured-output activities proposed by Lee and Van Patten (1995, 2003). The subjunctive was selected because of the processing principle (The Sentence Location Principle).

Benati (2005) conducted a similar and parallel classroom experiment investigating the effects of PI, TI and MOI on the acquisition of English simple past tense. The relevant processing principle in this case was the Lexical Preference Principle.

In all these studies where the primary effects of PI have been investigated and compared with two different types of output-based instruction (namely TI and MOI), the results have showed the following

(a) PI is a more effective approach to grammar instruction than TI and MOI as it seems to have a direct effect on learners' ability to process input (various processing problems, various linguistic forms, different languages and populations).

(b) PI also seems to provide learners with the ability to produce the target linguistic features during output practice. The PI groups performed as well as the TI and MOI groups on the production task and this is a remarkable finding given that subjects in the PI group were never asked to produce the target features through output practice.

Motivation of the present study

The present study focuses on the effects of PI model by assessing secondary effects (see Lee, 2004) of this approach of grammar instruction in the acquisition of two grammatical features of Japanese. As briefly reviewed in the previous paragraph and in Chapter 4 in this book, research on PI has so far focused on measuring its direct and primary effects by comparing this type of instruction with traditional and meaning-output based instruction. The results of the empirical research have shown that PI is a better approach to output-based approaches to grammar instruction. PI is very effective approach towards altering inappropriate processing strategies and instills appropriate ones in L2 learners.

Research measuring secondary effects for PI (Benati and Lee, 2008) has shown that learners receiving PI training in a form or structure affected by a processing principle would transfer those effects on a different form or structure affected by the same processing problem. Data exists in Italian, English and French. Despite the positive results obtained on measuring the secondary effects of PI, no research has yet been conducted to look into the secondary effects in the case of a non-European languages such as Japanese. In fact, as pointed out by Kanno (1999:1) studies on the acquisition of Japanese by foreign language learners are very limited and there is a clear need to expand 'the range of target languages whose acquisition is being investigated.'

The main aim of this study is to determine whether learners receiving PI can transfer that training on the acquisition of other forms affected by the same processing principle without further instruction. The data will be gathered in order to address the following questions:

(a) Will learners who receive training on one type of processing strategy for one specific form appropriately transfer the use of that strategy to other forms without further instruction in PI?

(b) After receiving instruction on the use of affirmative vs. negative present tense in Japanese, can learners process Japanese past tense morphology that is an inflection that appears in word final position?

The effects of PI practice have only been measured in isolation with individual strategies and linguistic features and therefore we are not aware of the possible training effects for a group of L2 learners who receive PI to alter a specific processing strategy. Therefore, this study extends previous research on secondary effects of PI on the acquisition of Japanese (see a review of these studies in Benati and Lee, 2008), by comparing the relative effects of two types of instructional interventions (PI vs. TI) on the secondary effects of PI on acquisition of Japanese past tense forms.

> ### Question to reflect on . . .
>
> What is the main purpose of this study? Please summarize main aims and objectives of the present classroom study.

Grammatical features

Japanese present tense morphology is an inflection that also appears in word final position. The morphology for affirmed verbs (-*masu*) is different from those for negated verbs (-*masen*). Standard Japanese word order places the verb (and its markings) in sentence final position. The semantic distinction between affirmative and negative verbal propositions is conveyed through word final, sentence final morphology. Learners will have to attend to the morphological difference between *shimasu* and *shimasen* to determine whether a proposition (studying) is affirmed or negated. This form is affected by the Sentence Location Principle.

The past tense marker is high in communicative value when it is the only indicator of tense. The marker's communicative value drops when it co-occurs with a lexical temporal indicator. The lexical temporal indicator makes the verb morphology redundant (P1c). Additionally, standard Japanese word order places the lexical temporal indicator in sentence initial position. It would be the first sentence element learners encounter whereas the verb morphology would be the last. In a sentence such as *Kinō kaisha ni ikimashita* (Yesterday, I went to the office) both the lexical item *Kinō* and the verb ending *ikimashita* communicate past tense. According to the 'Lexical Preference Principle' learners will naturally rely on the lexical item over the verb inflection in order to gather semantic information. The 'Lexical Preference Principle' has been investigated in many PI studies (e.g. Cadierno, 1995; Benati, 2001; Benati, 2004; Benati, 2005; Benati, Van Patten and Wong, 2005).

The grammatical feature of Japanese past tense was mainly selected because not only is it affected by the Lexical Preference Principle but also by the Sentence Location Principle as in the case of the first linguistic feature. According to Van Patten (2002), learners tend to process items in sentence initial position before those in final position and those in medial position. This processing strategy has been investigated in previous studies (Farley, 2001a, 2001b; Benati,

2005; see also Benati, Van Patten and Wong, 2005) and the effects of SIA have been proved vital in helping learners to circumvent this processing problem. Japanese past tense morphology is an inflection that appears in word final position (-*shita*). Japanese sentences end with verbs and the ending of the verb encodes the tense and also provides information on whether the sentence is positive or negative. Learners would tend to process elements in the initial position before elements in the final position according to Van Patten's principle, therefore they would skip over the grammatical marker and find it difficult to establish whether the sentence is positive or negative or whether it is referring to the present or the past. PI is designed to push learners to process the element in the final position that otherwise may not be processed and would lead to misinterpretation of the sentence. The main purpose of PI is to push learners to process the grammatical markers in the final position that otherwise may not be processed.

Research questions

Based on the motivation outlined in the previous section two specific questions were formulated:

Q1. Will there be any differences in how learners of Japanese exposed to two different types instructional treatments (PI vs. TI) interpret and produce sentences containing and expressing positive or negative present forms?

Q2. Will learners who receive training on one type of processing strategy for one specific form appropriately transfer the use of that strategy to other forms (namely past tense forms in Japanese) without further instruction in PI?

The first aim of this study was to compare the primary effects of PI and TI on the acquisition of a Japanese linguistic feature. The second aim was to measure the secondary effects of PI and particularly the training effects on a second Japanese linguistic feature affected by the same processing principles.

Design and procedure of the study

Participants and procedure

The experiment was designed to make the results as objective as possible within the constraints of a private Japanese language programme in Italy. Beginners students of Japanese participated in this study. All subjects were Italian native speakers and were studying Japanese in a private school were they received 4 hours of instruction over 2 consecutive days every week. The original sample of subjects (42) was reduced to 24 subjects (final data pool) as the participants went through a series of filters (e.g. subjects with previous knowledge in the two targeted linguistic features were not included in the final pool). The reduction of the original sample was also due to the effects of attrition. Participants who scored more than 60 percent were not included in the final data pool. The randomized and reduced sample consisted of three groups: PI group ($n = 9$); TI group ($n = 8$); C group ($n = 7$).

The randomization procedure used in this study allowed us to argue that any differences in the groups were due to the treatments because one can assume that other variables which might have affected the results exist in equal quantities in the three groups. Two different packs of materials (one for the PI group and one for the TI group) were produced for one of the two Japanese linguistic features by the researcher and used during the instructional treatments. The instructional materials were balanced in all ways (e.g. vocabulary, total number of activities) except the type of practice the students received (i.e. input versus output practice).

A pre- and post-test procedure was used with a control group and the two instructional treatments group. Participants were administered pre-tests in both linguistics features before the beginning of the instructional period (on the use of present forms and past forms) and post-tests immediately after the end of the instructional treatment (see Figure 7.1 for an overview of the experimental

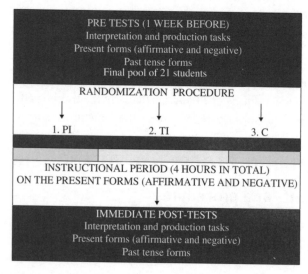

Figure 7.1 Overview of the experiments.

design used in the present study). Learners received the instructional treatments (4 hours in total, on 2 consecutive days) on the use of positive and negative present forms in Japanese. After the end of the instructional period, the groups were given post-tests on both the first instructed feature, and the second instructed feature (past tense forms) to measure for both primary and secondary effects.

The groups were taught by the same instructor (who was also the researcher) during the period of instruction.

Instructional treatments

Since the first aim of this study was to investigate the relative effects of two different types of instructional intervention on the acquisition of Japanese, two sets of materials were developed. One for the TI group which consisted in grammar teaching and output practice, and one for the PI group which consisted in teaching the subjects to process input sentences. The output-based activities required the subjects to produce accurately, present tense forms (affirmative and negative). The PI approach required learners to interpret sentences containing present tense forms (affirmative and negative), and make correct and appropriate form–meaning connections.

The two instructional treatments were balanced in terms of activity types, number of activities and use of visuals. Vocabulary was roughly the same and consisted in highly frequent and familiar items for Japanese language learners. The two treatments differed as to whether they were receptive or productive and both included explicit information about the targeted form. However, the explicit information provided to the PI group consisted in giving learners information about psycholinguistics processing problems involved in the grammatical form in focus in this study.

PI

The material was developed based on the guideline principles for the construction of structured input activities presented in Lee and Van Patten (1995). This input-based treatment consists of the use of SIA activities (referential and affective types) in which learners have to respond to the content sentences (see sample in Appendix A for the present tense) and some explicit information about the target form. Students belonging to this group were never asked to produce a sentence containing the targeted linguistic feature, but they were engaged in processing input sentences so that they could make better form–meaning connections and therefore interpret and comprehend the linguistic feature. In the present study, the input was 'structured' so that the grammatical forms carry a meaning and learners must attend to the form to complete the task.

In both studies, the input was 'structured' so that the grammatical forms carry a meaning and learners must attend to the form to complete the task. In the case of the use of positive vs. negative present forms, learners were required to pay attention to the verb in sentence final position to determine whether the meaning of the sentence was negative or positive.

TI

The second pack constructed for the TI treatment was prepared following the criteria of one approach to the teaching of grammar which involves the presentation of the present tense forms and the subsequent practice in how to make sentences in the present tense (affirmative and negative forms). The activities used for the implementation of this approach were constructed to make learners practise by producing the forms at sentence level. Some of those activities lacked of any referential meaning.

This output-based treatment (see a sample in Appendix B for the present tense) had the following characteristics: presentations of forms, which was followed by the use of activities in which learners have to practise producing the correct forms.

Control group

The control group received no instruction on the target features but was subjected to a comparable amount of exposure to the target language for the same amount of time.

Assessment

Four tests (see Appendix C for the assessment task for the present tense and Appendix D for the assessment task of the past tense forms) were produced: one for the interpretation task and one for the production task for both instructional features. The fact that both interpretation and production tasks were present in all the tests is clear evidence that neither instructional group was favoured. An interpretation task was used as a measure of knowledge gained at interpreting present tense (affirmative vs. negative) and one developed and used to measure student's knowledge to interpret past tense forms at sentence level.

In the case of the interpretation test for the present tense, ten sentences (five affirmative and five negative) were used, and participants had to rely on the verb (in final position) to establish whether the sentence was negative or affirmative.

In the case of the past tense forms, temporal adverbs were removed from the sentences so that the learners' attention was directed towards the verb endings as indicators of tense. Learners should use verbal morphology as an indicator of tense since the lexical indicators of tense were absent. The interpretation test consisted of 20 aural sentences (ten in the present which served as distracters and ten in the past) in which temporal adverbs and subject nouns or pronouns were removed, so that the participants could not rely on those elements to assign tenses but had to focus on verb morphology as the only indicator to establish when the action was taking place (present vs. past).

The tests were presented to the subjects on a tape player. No repetition was provided so that the test would measure real-time comprehension. In the interpretation task, the raw scores were calculated as follows: incorrect response = 0 point, correct response = 1point. In the present study, only the past sentences were counted for the raw scores for a maximum score of 10.

Written completion production tasks were developed and used to measure learner's ability to produce sentences in the past forms and the use of positive and negative sentences in present forms. In the case of the positive vs. negative present forms, the written production grammar test consisted of ten sentences to complete (five affirmative and five negative) in the present form. In the written production tasks (past tense forms) learners were required to complete a text producing ten correct past forms in Japanese. The written completion production task was developed and used to measure learner's ability to produce sentences in the past forms. In the written production tasks (past tense forms) learners were required to complete a text producing ten correct past forms in Japanese. The scoring procedure in the production task was calculated as follows: fully correct form = 1 point; incorrect = 0 point.

Question to reflect on . . .

How is this study designed in terms of subjects, materials and overall procedures? What type of design was used?

Results

Primary effects (positive vs. negative in present forms)

Interpretation data

Data were collected for the interpretation task to measure primary effects of the instructional treatments. A pre-test was used and administered to the participants some time before the beginning of the experiment. A one-way ANOVA conducted on the pre-test alone revealed no significant differences among the two class means before instruction ($p = .987$). A repeated measures ANOVA was used on the raw scores of the interpretation task to establish the possible effects of instruction on the way learners interpret sentences containing present forms in Japanese (affirmative vs. negative). The results graphically presented in Graph 7.1 show that there is a significant effect for Instruction ($F(2, 24) = 95.344$, $p = .000$). There was significant effect for Time ($F(2, 24) = 108.527$, $p = .000$) and for interaction between Instruction and Time ($F(4, 24) = 193.863$, $p = .000$). The means in Table 7.1 indicate that the PI group made greater gain than the TI group and the control group. The Scheffe post-hoc tests revealed the following contrasts: the PI group was significantly different from the TI group ($p = .000$) and the control group ($p = .000$); the TI group and the control group were not different ($p = .339$). PI as a type of instruction had positive and statistically significant primary effects on how participants interpret sentences containing the affirmative vs. negative present tense forms. Those effects are significantly better that the other instructional treatment and the control group.

The Scheffe post-hoc tests revealed the following contrasts: the PI group was significantly different from the TI group ($p = .000$) and the control group ($p = .000$); the TI group and the control group were not different ($p = .339$).

Table 7.1 Means and standard deviation for interpretation task pre-test and post-test (present). Primary effects

		Pre-test		Post-test	
Variable	n	Mean	SD	Mean	SD
PI	9	.733	.318	6.888	1.166
TI	8	.875	.356	.925	.246
C	7	.485	.112	.302	.173

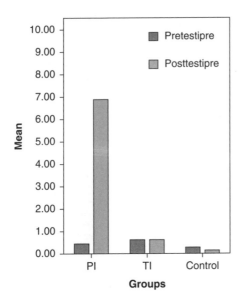

Production data

A written production task was administered to the three groups. As in the case of the interpretation data statistical analyses were performed on the raw scores of the written task. A pre-test, administered to the subjects some time before the beginning of the experiment revealed no statistically significant difference between the groups ($p = .571$). A repeated measures ANOVA used to establish the possible effects of the three groups on the way learners produce written sentences to express affirmative vs. negative present tense forms in Japanese, indicated significant main effects for instruction ($F(2, 24) = 138.183$, $p = .000$) that there was a significant effect for Time ($F(2, 24) = 35.960$, $p = .000$). There was significant interaction between Instruction and Time ($F(4, 24) = 248.050$, $p = .250$). The means showed in Table 7.2 and graphically in Graph 7.2 indicate

Table 7.2 Means and standard deviation for production task pre-test and post-test (present). Primary effects

Variable	n	Pre-test		Post-test	
		Mean	SD	Mean	SD
PI	9	.333	.118	4.388	1.166
TI	8	.2575	.356	4.725	1.246
C	7	.642	.214	.485	.114

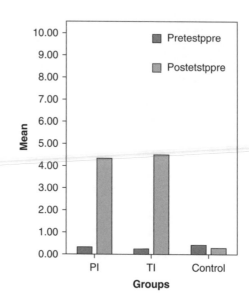

that the PI groups and TI groups made similar gains from pre- to post-tests. Both treatments seem to bring about the same improved performance on producing Japanese present tense forms at sentence level.

The Scheffe post-hoc tests revealed the following contrasts: the PI group was significantly different from the control group ($p = .000$); the TI group was significantly better than the control group ($p = .004$); the PI group and the TI group were not different ($p = .987$).

Secondary effects (past tense forms)

Interpretation data

Data were collected for the interpretation task to measure possible secondary effects. This is in order to establish whether there were any possible training effects on the groups receiving PI. The pre-test, administered to the three groups, some time before the beginning of the experiment revealed no statistically significant difference between the groups ($p = .346$). A repeated measures ANOVA was used on the raw scores of the interpretation task to establish the possible effects of instruction and no instruction on the way learners interpret sentences where the past tense in Japanese is only expressed by verb morphology. The results graphically presented in Graph 7.3. show that there is a significant effect for Instruction (F(2, 24) = 75.425, $p = .000$); that there was a significant effect for Time (F(2, 24) = 37.799, $p = .000$); and there was

Table 7.3 Means and standard deviation for interpretation task pre-test and post-test (past). Secondary effects

		Pre-test		Post-test	
Variable	n	Mean	SD	Mean	SD
PI	9	.433	.118	4.288	1.166
TI	8	.675	.356	1.125	.246
C	7	.192	.214	.485	.114

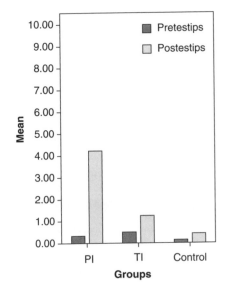

significant interaction between Instruction and Time ($F(4, 24) = 122.253$, $p = .000$). The means in Table 7.3 indicate that the PI group made greater gain than the TI and control group.

The post-hoc tests revealed the following contrasts: the PI group was significantly different from the TI group ($p = .000$); the PI group was also better than the control group ($p = .000$); the TI group and the control group were not different ($p = .103$).

PI is a type of instruction that has secondary effects on the way learners process forms affected by the same processing problem.

Production data

A written production task was also administered to the three groups to measure secondary effects on the ability to produce past tense forms in Japanese.

A pre-test, administered to the three groups, some time before the beginning of the experiment revealed no statistically significant difference between the groups ($p = .219$). As in the case of the interpretation data, statistical analysis was performed on the raw scores of the written completion text. A repeated measure ANOVA was used on the raw scores of the production task to establish the possible effects of instruction and no instruction on the way learners produce sentences containing past tense forms. The results graphically presented in Graph 7.4, show significant effect for Instruction ($F(2, 24) = 14.157$, $p = .001$); that there was a significant effect for Time ($F(2, 24) = 9.352$, $p = .001$); and there was significant interaction between Instruction and Time ($F(4, 24) = 104.483$, $p = .000$). The means showed in Table 7.4 and graphically in Graph 7.4 indicate that the PI groups and TI groups made similar equal gains.

Table 7.4 Means and standard deviation for production task pre-test and post-test (past). Secondary effects

Variable	n	Pre-test		Post-test	
		Mean	SD	Mean	SD
PI	9	.333	.148	2.388	1.166
TI	8	1.175	.356	1.725	1.246
C	7	.142	.214	.085	.114

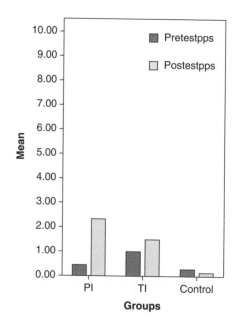

PI seems to have secondary effects learners' performance on producing Japanese past tense forms at sentence level task.

The post-hoc tests revealed the following contrasts: the PI group was not significantly different from the TI group ($p = .821$); the PI group was better than the control group ($p = .000$); the TI group was also better than the control group ($p = .001$).

PI is a type of instruction that has secondary effects on the way learners process forms affected by the same processing problem.

Summary of results

Based on previous research it was hypothesized (Q1.) that the group who received PI would perform better in the interpretation task than the TI group on the present tense forms (affirmative vs. negative). The instructional data collected through the interpretation and production task and the subsequent statistical analysis revealed that the differences among the two groups under investigation were statistically significant as far as the interpretation task. The PI group's performance was better than that of the TI group and the control group in the interpretation task. Both the PI and the TI group performed equally in the production task. The results confirm primary positive effects for PI as a type of grammar instruction.

On the basis of previous research it was also hypothesized (Q2.) that the subjects receiving PI would transfer the training on the processing principles related to the present tense forms to another form affected by the same principles, namely the past test forms in Japanese. The results revealed that the PI group performs better than the other two groups on the interpretation task and the two instructional groups performance was very similar in the production task. The results confirmed previous results on the cumulative and secondary effects of PI (Benati and Lee, 2008).

> ### Questions to reflect on . . .
>
> What type of data collection and data analysis were used?
> What are the main results?

Discussion and conclusion

The results of the interpretation data in both experimental studies, although parallel to those obtained by other studies investigating the primary effects of

PI on a perceptual strategy in different romance languages, expand previous findings and provide a welcome addition to the continuing investigation on the effects of PI in two linguistic features of Japanese. The evidence collected in this study have shown that PI is a better instructional treatment than TI practice as showed in previous studies (see for a full review Lee 2004; Lee and Benati, 2007a, 2007b) and the positive primary effects of PI are generalizable to the acquisition of present tense form in Japanese. In addition to that, the results from this study have provided evidence that PI has indeed secondary effects on L2 learners and these effects are measurable on a linguistic feature (past tense forms) of Japanese.

The participants who received PI were able to perform significantly better than the TI group in the interpretation task in both linguistic features. The two instructional groups equally improved their performance in the production tasks in both linguistic features. The latter finding is extremely important if we consider that the group receiving PI was never involved in activities in which they had to produce the target features.

Despite the fact that the PI groups were not familiar with the production task, they were able to perform at least as well as the TI group. This particular finding provides further evidence of the impact of PI on learners' developing system on a different language (Japanese).

The findings from this study confirm previous findings measuring secondary effects of PI (Benati and Lee, 2008) as learners in the PI group outperformed the TI group in both interpretation measures. The participants in the PI group were able to transfer the training received on the present tense forms when they were asked to interpret sentences containing past tense forms. Learners who were trained to pay attention to the verbal morphology forms to interpret the meaning of the sentence were able to make better meaning form connections and process the input correctly and more efficiently. Learners in the PI group were also able to transfer their training on one processing principle (Sentence Location Principle) to another processing principle (Lexical Preference Principle). Training subjects on one processing problem through PI is transferable to other forms affected by the same or similar processing problem without further instruction. PI practice on one particular processing problem produce some effects on a different processing problem. Learners trained on the Sentence Location Principle might be able to transfer the use of this strategy to other forms affected by the Lexical Preference Principle without any further instruction in PI.

The main outcome from this study is that it reaffirms the positive effects of PI in altering learners' processing principles, transfer positively this training and consequently have an effect on learners' developing system. Research on PI has clearly indicated that this input-based approach offers more instructional benefits than output practice. Lee and Van Patten (1995) have rightly argued that 'traditional instruction which is intended to cause a change in the developing system, is akin to putting the cart before the horse when it comes to acquisition; the learner is asked to produce when the developing system has not yet had a chance to build up a representation of the language based on input data' (p. 95). Van Patten (2003:27) has strongly argued that output practice is not responsible for the making of an implicit system.

The findings from of this study have repercussions at empirical and theoretical levels. At the empirical level, the findings from this study provide evidence on the generalizability and effectiveness of PI primary and secondary effects on the acquisition of another language (Japanese) among beginner learners of a different L1: namely Italian.

As far as the theoretical level is concerned, the contribution of the present study is that it contributes directly to the discussion on the crucial role that input processing plays in SLA. In respect of this, the results provide further support for current models of SLA (Van Patten, 1996, 2002, 2004) which link input processing and the developing system.

Limitations and further research

Despite the positive outcomes of this investigation, there are some limitations that further research should address. The first one is related to the relatively small number of subjects who took part in the experiment. Further research should replicate the study with a larger population.

A second limitation of the present studies is that instructional effects were measured in an immediate post-test battery only. Hence, the longer-term effects of PI and its components on the acquisition of the grammatical feature of the present study should be re-investigated. Further research should be carried out to compare secondary effects of PI in the acquisition of different linguistic features in Japanese by measuring discourse level interpretation and production tasks (Benati and Lee, 2008) as secondary effects have only focused on sentence level tasks. Further research should ensure that transfer of training is the only observable variable responsible for improved knowledge of non-targeted linguistics feature.

Further research must make sure that no other variables can accounted for the positive learning outcomes obtained in this study.

Further research should also investigate the transfer of training effects on other linguistics features of Japanese which are captured by different processing principles so that we can generalize the findings of the present study.

Question to reflect on . . .

How did the researcher interpret the results? Are there any other limitations and areas for further research?

More questions to reflect on . . .

(1) What are the main findings? Has this study provided an answer to the questions raised?
(2) Can we consider this study valid and reliable? If Yes, Why?
(3) What is the next step? Can you indicate other possible avenues for further research in Japanese in this area?
(4) Can you read the following study in Japanese ('Directing learners' attention to sentence final position.' In Lee, J. F., Benati, A. G. 2007(b). *Second Language processing: An analysis of Theory, Problems and Possible Solutions (111–125).* London: Continuum) and identify the following:

  (1) Research question/motivation of the study
  (2) Subjects
  (3) Method
  (4) Type of data
  (5) Type of analysis
  (6) Main findings

Key terms

Analysis of Variance (ANOVA): this is a statistical procedure used to measure the difference between the mean of two or more groups.

Assessment (tests): in an experimental study, this is the dependent variable used to measure the effects of the independent variable (instructional treatment/s).

Mean (M): this refers to the average of a set of scores.

Participants (population): a group of individuals, selected and chosen for an experiment, who share similar characteristics.

Post-hoc analysis: statistical analysis used to establish which groups have significant different value for the mean.

Treatment (s): in an experimental study, this refers to a method/technique whose effectiveness is to be measured. It is the independent variable in an experimental study.

Further reading

A., Lee, J. (2008). *Grammar Acquisition and Processing Instruction: Secondary and Cumulative Effects.* Clevedon: Multilingual Matters.

Benati, A. and Lee, J. (2009). *Processing Instruction and Discourse.* London: Continuum.

Conclusion

The purpose of this book was to reflect on some major topics related to language acquisition and CLT teaching in order to provide an alternative way to teach Japanese as a second language. The main aim of this book was to help existing and future teachers of Japanese to have a better understanding as to what CLT approach really is and how it can be implemented in the language classroom (in Chapter 4 we use Lee and Van Patten (1995, 2003) theories and practices in language teaching to provide a framework for CLT in Japanese). The book also provides readers with explanation as to why at theoretical level (findings in instructed L2 research reviewed in Chapter 1 and 2), the CLT approach is justified as an approach to teach a foreign language such as Japanese.

Research findings in SLA have revealed the limited role of instruction. However, this does not mean that in a communicative approach to language teaching, teachers should renounce teaching the language. The creation of learners' implicit system is input driven and therefore instructors should provide comprehensible and meaning-bearing input in the classroom. Input and communicative interactions should be encouraged from the beginning level of learning. The idea is to create a classroom where communication is the main goal for instruction and learners are involved in communicative tasks where meaning and message are on focus in a input-rich environment. This type of communicative practice should also be directed to the learners' acquisition of grammar and vocabulary. Grammar should not be taught in a traditional way following a sequence which goes from the explicit and paradigmatic explanation of forms/structures to output mechanical practice. Grammar should be taught keeping in mind that the role of input is paramount in developing grammatical competence. The type of grammar teaching we advocate considers the way learners process input and offers opportunities for learners to make better form-meaning connections. In this book we have proved that this approach to grammar instruction is successful in teaching Japanese grammar.

We have argued that learners after the input stage should be engaged in communicative tasks where they need to produce language for the purpose of expressing some meaning. Learners must use the language to obtain information and do something with the information they have obtained. We have provided guidelines and examples to produce communicative tasks in Japanese for developing learners' listening, speaking, writing and reading comprehension skills.

To summarize, in our suggestions for a more communicative approach to teach Japanese to L2 learners we have recommended the following:

(a) expose learners to refined, comprehensible and meaning-bearing input;
(b) develop grammar tasks where learners can process the linguistics characteristics of a target language in the input (structured input activities);
(c) develop communicative grammar tasks using a variety of techniques (e.g. structured input activities, textual enhancement, consciousness rising) that provide at the same time a focus on form and a focus on meaning.
(d) develop communicative tasks that encourage learners to produce the language for a meaningful purpose through interactive tasks and other tasks where the focus is on grammar (e.g. structured output activities);
(e) develop communicative tasks that encourage interactions which focus on meaning (e.g. task-based activities, role-plays).

Teachers of Japanese must take up this challenge and make their classroom more communicative. At the same time one of the other main aims of this book was to provide a platform for teachers of Japanese to get involved in classroom and experimental research. We have provided a possible experimental framework to help teachers engaging in this kind of research. The final chapter is an example of how research on the effects of a specific focus on form called processing instruction can provide some practical implications for the teaching of Japanese grammar. The hope is that more students and teachers can take this challenge forward.

Appendices

PI Treatment on Japanese Present Affirmative vs. Negative

Structured input activities

Attività A

Ascolta e determina se la frase è affermativa o negativa. Presta attenzione al verbo in posizione finale!

	Koutei 肯定	Hitei 否定
1.	☐	☐
2.	☐	☐
3.	☐	☐
4.	☐	☐
5.	☐	☐

Sentences heard by learner:

1. *Watashi wa italiago o benkyou shimasu*   私はイタリア語を勉強します。
2. *Watashi wa italiago o benkyou shimasen*   私はイタリア語を勉強しません。
3. *Watashi wa London ni sumimasu*   私はロンドンに住みます。
4. *Watashi wa London ni sumimasen*   私はロンドンに住みません。
5. *Watashi wa gekijyou ni ikimasen*   私は劇場に行きません。

Attività B

Ascolta le frasi riguardo alle abitudini di uno studente. Decidi se sono affermative o negative e poi stabilisci se sei in accordo o in disaccordo.

	Koutei 肯定	Hitei 否定	Hai	Iie
1.	☐	☐		
2.	☐	☐		
3.	☐	☐		
4.	☐	☐		
5.	☐	☐		

Sentences heard by learner:

1. *Watashi wa tomodachi to dekakemasu*   私は友達と出かけます。
2. *Watashi wa tomodachi to dekakemasen*   私は友達と出かけません。
3. *Watashi wa gekijyou ni ikimasu*   私は劇場に行きます。
4. *Watashi wa John to hanashimasen*   私はジョンと話しません。

Il presente in frase affermativa si forma con il suffisso *–masu* mentre in frase negative con il suffisso *-masen*). Memorizza i seguenti verbi al presente (forme positive e negative)

Appendix B
TI Treatment on Japanese
Present Affirmative vs. Negative

Traditional instruction

Attività A

Trasforma le frasi dall'italiano al giapponese secondo l'esempio:

Io gioco a tennis/Io non gioco a tennis
watashi wa tenisu o shimasu
watashi wa tenisu o shimasen

1. Io torno a casa presto/Io non torno a casa presto
2. Io parlo il giapponese/Io non parlo il giapponese
3. Io guaro la TV/Io non guardo la TV
4. Io ascolto la radio/Io non ascolto la radio
5. Io prendo l'autobus alle 3/Io non prendo l'autobus alle tre

Attività B

Cambia le frasi dall'affermativa alla negativa

(1) Watashi wa John to hanashimasu   私はジョンと話します。
(2) Watashi wa nihongo de shimbum o yomimasu   私は日本語で新聞を読みます。
(3) Watashi wa gimu ni ikimasu   私はジムに行きます。
(4) Watashi wa gengogaku o benkyou shimasu   私は言語学を勉強します。
(5) Watashi wa ronbun o kakimasu   私は論文を書きます。

Explicit information for traditional instruction

Il presente in frase affermativa si forma con il suffisso –*masu* mentre in frase negative con il suffisso -*masen*). Memorizza i seguenti verbi al presente (forme positive e negative)

Forme del presente	
Affermativa	**Negativa**
Ikimasu (vado) 行きます	ikimasen (non vado) 行きません
Kimasu (vengo) 来ます	kimasen (non vengo) 来ません
Kaerimasu (ritorno)帰ります	
kaerimasen (non ritorno) 帰りません	
Mimasu (vedo) 見ます	mimasen (non vedo) 見ません
Kikimasu (ascolto) 聞きます	
kikimasen (non acolto)聞きません	
Tabemasu (mangio) 食べます	
abemasen (non mangio)食べません	
Nonimasu (bevo)飲みませ	
nominasen (non bevo)飲みません	
Kaimasu (compro)買います	
kaimasen (non compro)買いません	
Yomimasu (leggo)読みます	
yominasen (non leggo)読みません	
Shimasu (studio) します	
shimasen (non studio)しません	

Appendix C
Tests for Japanese Present Affirmative vs. Negative

Interpretation task

Ascolta le frasi riguardo alle abitudini di uno studente e stabilisci se si tratta di una frase affermativa o positiva al presente.

1	☐ Koutei	☐ Hitei	☐ Wakarimasen
2	☐ Koutei	☐ Hitei	☐ Wakarimasen
3	☐ Koutei	☐ Hitei	☐ Wakarimasen
4	☐ Koutei	☐ Hitei	☐ Wakarimasen
5	☐ Koutei	☐ Hitei	☐ Wakarimasen
6	☐ Koutei	☐ Hitei	☐ Wakarimasen
7	☐ Koutei	☐ Hitei	☐ Wakarimasen
8	☐ Koutei	☐ Hitei	☐ Wakarimasen
9	☐ Koutei	☐ Hitei	☐ Wakarimasen
10	☐ Koutei	☐ Hitei	☐ Wakarimasen
11	☐ Koutei	☐ Hitei	☐ Wakarimasen
12	☐ Koutei	☐ Hitei	☐ Wakarimasen
13	☐ Koutei	☐ Hitei	☐ Wakarimasen
14	☐ Koutei	☐ Hitei	☐ Wakarimasen
15	☐ Koutei	☐ Hitei	☐ Wakarimasen
16	☐ Koutei	☐ Hitei	☐ Wakarimasen
17	☐ Koutei	☐ Hitei	☐ Wakarimasen
18	☐ Koutei	☐ Hitei	☐ Wakarimasen
19	☐ Koutei	☐ Hitei	☐ Wakarimasen
20	☐ Koutei	☐ Hitei	☐ Wakarimasen

Sentences heard by lesarners:

1. *Watashi wa tomodachi to dekakemasu*　　私は友達と出かけます。
2. *Watashi wa tomodachi to dekakemasen*　　私は友達と出かけません。
3. *Shumatsu tomodachi to sugoshimashita*　　週末、友達と過ごしました。
4. *Watashi wa terebi o mimasen*　　私はテレビを見ません。
5. *totemo ii hon o yomishamita*　　とてもいい本を読みました。
6. *Joan to gekijyou ni ikimashita*　　ジョアンと劇場に行きました。
7. *Watashi wa terebi o mimasu*　　私はテレビを見ます。
8. *ronbun o kakimashita*　　論文を書きました。
9. *nohongo de shinbun o yomimasen*　　日本語で新聞を読みません。
10. *uchi/ie ni kaerimashita*　　家に帰りました。
11. *san-ji ni basu ni norimasen*　　3時にバスに乗りません。
12. *uchi/ie ni kaerimashita*　　家に帰りました。
13. *watashi wa Alessandro to hanashimasu*　　私はアレッサンドロと話します。
14. *Bernie to hanashimashita*　　Bernieと話しました。
15. *watashi wa gimu ni ikimasen*　　私はジムに行きません。
16. *watashi wa gimu ni ikimashita*　　私はジムに行きました。
17. *watashi wa gekijyou ni ikimasu*　　私は劇場に行きます。
18. *Kinou watashi wa john to kouen o arukimashita*　　昨日、私はジョンと公園を歩きました。
19. *gengogaku o benkyou shimasu*　　言語学を勉強します。
20. *bar de wain o takusan*　　バーでワインをたくさん？

Production task

Completa le seguenti frasi al presente

1. Watashi wa Italia ni -------------- (vado).　　私はイタリアに
2. Watashi wa Italia ni -------------- (non vado).　　私はイタリアに
3. Watashi wa mainichi tenisu o -------------- (gioco).　　私は毎日テニスを
4. Watashi wa mainichi tenisu o -------------- (non gioco).　　私は毎日テニスを
5. Watashi wa maiban tereibi o -------------- (non guardo).　　私は毎晩テレビを
6. Watashi wa denwa de Paul to -------------- (parlo).　　私は電話てポールと
7. Watashi wa denwa de Paul to -------------- (non parlo).　　私は電話てポールと
8. Watashi wa mainichi osoku made -------------- (dormo).　　私は毎日遅くまで
9. Watashi wa rajio o -------------- (ascolto).　　私はラジオを
10. Watashi wa rajio o -------------- (non ascolto).　　私はラジオを

Tests for the Past Tense Forms

Interpretation task

Ascolta le frasi e stabilisci quando avviene l'azione

1	☐	Kyonen	去年	☐ Maitoshi	毎年
2	☐	Kyonen		☐ Maitoshi	
3	☐	Kinō	昨日	☐ Mainichi	毎日
4	☐	Kinō		☐ Mainichi	
5	☐	Kinō		☐ Maiban	毎晩
6	☐	Kinō		☐ Maiban	
7	☐	Sakuban	昨晩	☐ Mainichi	
8	☐	Sakuban		☐ Mainichi	
9	☐	Kinō		☐ Mainichi	
10	☐	Kynō		☐ Mainichi	
11	☐	Kyonen		☐ Maitoshi	
12	☐	Kyonen		☐ Maitoshi	
13	☐	Kinō		☐ Mainichi	
14	☐	Kinō		☐ Mainichi	
15	☐	Kinō		☐ Maiban	
16	☐	Kinō		☐ Maiban	
17	☐	Sakuban		☐ Mainichi	
18	☐	Sakuban		☐ Mainichi	
19	☐	Kinō		☐ Mainichi	
20	☐	Kynō		☐ Mainichi	

Sentence heard by learners:

1. *italia ni ikimashita*   イタリアに行きました。
2. *italia ni ikimasu*   イタリアに行きます。
3. *tenisu o shimashita*   テニスをしました。
4. *tenisu o shimasu*   テニスをします。

5. *ii eiga o mimashita* いい映画を見ました。
6. *terebi o mimasu* テレビを見ます。
7. *osoku made nete imashita* 遅くまで寝ていました。
8. *osoku made nemasu* 遅くまで寝ます。
9. *de Paul to hanashimashita* ポールと話しました。
   in this position of de doesn't make sense
10. *de Paul to hanashimasu* ポールと話します。
11. *gekijyou ni ikimashita* 劇場に行きました。
12. *no shumatsu tomodachi to sugoshimashita* 週末、友達と過ごしました。
    in this position of no doesn't make sense
13. *restouran de hatarakimasu* レストランで働きます。
14. *John to kouen o arukimashita* ジョンと公園を歩きました。
15. *gakkou de nihongo o benkyou shimashita* 学校で日本語を勉強しました。
16. *marason o shimashita* マラソンをしました。
17. *totemo ii hon o yomimasu* とてもいい本を読みます。
18. *Paul to kouen o arukimasu* ポールと公園を歩きます。
19. *Jon to hanashimasu* ジョンと話します。
20. *uchi/ie ni kaeriimasu* 家に帰ります。

Production task (sample)

Completa le seguenti frasi al passato

1. Kinō rajio o -------------- (ascoltato). 昨日、ラジオを
2. Kinō tenisu o -------------- (giocato). 昨日、テニスを
3. Kinō italiago o benkyou -------------- (studiato). 昨日、イタリア語を勉強
4. Kinō terebi o -------------- (guardato). 昨日、テレビを
5. Kinō italia ni -------------- (andato). 昨日、イタリアに
6. Kinō rajio o -------------- (studiato). 昨日、ラジオを
7. Kinō italiago o -------------- (insegnato). 昨日、イタリア語を
8. Kinō totemo osuku ni -------------- (andato a letto). 昨日、とても遅くに

References

Allwright, D. (1988). *Observation in the Language Classroom.* London: Longman.

Anderson, J. (1983). *The Architecture of Cognition.* Harvard: Harvard University Press.

Bacham, L. F. and Palmer, A. S. (1996). *Language Testing in Practice.* Oxford: OUP.

Benati, A. (2001). A comparative study on the effects of processing instruction and output-based instruction on the acquisition of the Italian future tense. *Language Teaching Research 5,* 95–127.

Benati, A. (2004a). The effects of structured input and explicit information on the acquisition of Italian future tense. In B. Van Patten (Ed.). *Processing Instruction: Theory, Research, and Commentary* (pp. 207–255). Mahwah, NJ: Lawrence Erlbaum Associates.

Benati, A. (2004b). The effects of processing instruction and its components on the acquisition of gender agreement in Italian. *Language Awareness,* 13, 67–80.

Benati, A. (2005). The effects of PI, TI and MOI in the acquisition of English simple past tense. *Language Teaching Research,* 9, 67–113.

Benati, A., Lee, J. (2008). *Grammar Acquisition and Processing Instruction: Secondary and Cumulative Effects.* Clevedon: Multilingual Matters.

Benati, A. and Peressini, R. (1998). *Ritocchi.* Greenwich: Greenwich University Press.

Benati, A. and Lee, J. (2009). *Processing Instruction and Discourse.* London: Continuum.

Benati, A., Van Patten, B. and Wong, W. (2005). *Input Processing and Processing Instruction.* Rome: Armando Editore.

Bialystok, E. (1982). On the relationship between knowing and using forms. *Applied Linguistics,* 3, 181–206.

Breen, M. and Candlin, C. (1980). The essentials of a communicative curriculum in language teaching. *Applied Linguistics,* 1, 1–47.

Brumfit, C. (1984). *Communicative Methodology in Language Teaching.* Cambridge: CUP.

Bygate, M., Skehan, P. and Swain, M. (Eds) (2001). *Researching Pedagogic Tasks Second Language Learning, Teaching and Testing.* Harlow: Pearson Education.

Cadierno, T. (1995). Formal instruction from a processing perspective: an investigation into the Spanish past tense. *The Modern Language Journal,* 79, 179–93.

Campbell, D. and Stanley, J. (1963). *Handbook on Research on Teaching.* Chicago, IL: Rand McNelly.

Canale, M. and Swain, M. (1980). Theoretical bases of communicative approaches to second language teaching and testing. *Applied Linguistics,* 1, 1: 1–47.

Caroll, S. (2001). *Input and Evidence: The Raw Material of Second Language Acquisition.* Amsterdam: John Benjamins.

Carroll, J. and Swain, M. (1993). The role of feedback in adult second language acquisition: error correction and morphological generalizations. *Applied Psycholinguistics*, 13, 173–98.

Chaudron, C. (1988). *Second Language Classroom: Research on Teaching and Learning*. Cambridge: CUP.

Cheng, A. (2004). Processing instruction and Spanish *ser* and *estar* forms with semantic-aspectual value. In B. Van Patten (Ed.). *Processing Instruction: Theory, Research and Commentary* (pp. 119–141). Mahwah, NJ: Lawrence Erlbaum Associates.

Chikamatsu, N. (2003). Recent Research in Reading Japanese as a Foreign Language. In Y. A. Hatasa, (Ed.). *An invitation to SLA research* (pp. 187–205). Tokyo: Kurosio Publisher.

Chomsky, N. (1965). *Aspects of the Theory of Syntax*. Cambridge, MA: MIT Press.

Chomsky, N. (1975). *Reflections on Language*. New York: Pantheon Books.

Corder, P. (1967). The significance of learners' errors. *International Review of Applied Linguistics*, 5, 161–169.

Corder, P. (1981). *Error Analysis and Interlanguage*. Oxford: OUP.

Di Biase, B. and Kawaguchi, S. (2002). Exploring the typological plausibility of processability theory: language development in Italian second language and Japanese second language. *Second Language Research*, 18, 274–302.

DeKeyser, R. (1995). Learning second language grammar rules: an experiment. with a miniature linguistic system. *Studies in Second Language Acquisition*, 17, 379–410.

DeKeyser, R. (Ed.). (2006). *Practicing in a second language: Perspectives from applied linguistics and cognitive psychology*. New York: CUP.

Doughty, C. (1991). Second language instruction does make a difference. *Studies in Second Language Acquisition*, 13, 431–69.

Doughty, C. (1999). The psycholinguistics plausibility or recasts. Paper presented at the 12th World Congress of Applied Linguistics, Tokyo.

Doughty, C. and E. Varela (1998). Communicative focus on form. In C. Doughty and J. Williams (Eds). *Focus on Form in Classroom Second Language Acquisition*. Cambridge: CUP.

Doughty, C. and Williams, J. (Eds) (1998). *Focus on Form in Classroom Second Language Acquisition*. Cambridge: CUP.

Dulay, H. C. and Burt, M. K. (1974). Natural sequences in child second language acquisition. *Language Learning*, 24, 37–53.

Ellis, N. (2002). Frequency effects in language processing: a review with implications for theories of implicit and explicit language acquisition. *Studies in Second Language Acquisition*, 24, 143–188.

Ellis, N. (2003). Constructions, chunking, and connectionism: the emergence of second language structure. In C. Doughty and M. H. Long (Eds). *The Handbook of Second Language Acquisition* (pp. 63–103). Oxford: Blackwell Publishing.

Ellis, R. (1990). *Instructed Second Language Acquisition*. Oxford: Blackwell.

Ellis, R. (1991). Grammar teaching practice or consciousness raising? In R. Ellis (Ed.). *Second Language Acquisition and Second Language Pedagogy* (pp. 232–241). Clevedon: Multilingual Matters.

Ellis, R. (1994). *The Study of Second Language Acquisition*. Oxford: OUP.

Ellis, R. (1997). *SLA research and language teaching.* Oxford: OUP.

Ellis, R. (2003). *Task-Based Language Learning and Teaching.* Oxford: OUP.

Everson, M. and Kuriya, Y. (1999). An exploratory study into the reading strategies of learners of Japanese as a foreign language. *Journal of the Association of Teachers of Japanese, 32,* 1–21.

Farley, A. (2004a). The relative effects of processing instruction and meaning-based output instruction. In B. Van Patten (Ed.). *Processing Instruction: Theory, Research and Commentary* (pp. 143–168). Mahwah, NJ: Lawrence Erlbaum Associates.

Farley, A. P. (2001a). The effects of processing instruction and meaning-based output instruction. *Spanish Applied Linguistics, 5,* 57–94.

Farley, A. P. (2001b). Authentic processing instruction and the Spanish subjunctive. *Hispania, 84,* 289–299.

Farley, A. (2004b). Processing instruction and the Spanish subjunctive: is explicit information needed? In B. Van Patten (Ed.). *Processing Instruction: Theory, Research and Commentary* (pp. 227–239). Mahwah, NJ: Lawrence Erlbaum Associates.

Farley, A. (2005). *Structured Input: Grammar Instruction for the Acquisition-Oriented Classroom.* New York: McGraw-Hill.

Felix, S. (1981). The effect of formal instruction on second language acquisition. *Language Learning, 31,* 87–112.

Flower, L. and Hayes, J. R. (1981). A cognitive process theory of writing. *College Composition and Communication, 32,* 365–87.

Fotos, S. (1993). Consciousness-raising and noticing through focus on form: grammar task performance versus formal instruction. *Applied Linguistics, 14,* 385–407.

Fotos, S. and Ellis, R. (1991). Communicating about grammar: a task-based approach. *TESOL Quarterly, 25,* 605–28.

Gass, S. (1988). Integrating research areas: a framework for second language studies. *Applied Linguistics, 9,* 198–217.

Gass, S. (1997). *Input, Interaction and the Second Language Learner.* Mahwah, NJ: Lawrence Erlbaum Associates.

Gass, S. and Selinker, L. (2001). *Second Language Acquisition: An Introductory Course.* Mahwah, NJ: Lawrence Erlbaum Associates.

Halliday, M. A. K. (1973). *Language in a Social Perspective. Explorations in the Functions of Language.* London: Edward Arnold.

Haneda, M. (1996). Peer interaction in an adult second language class: an analysis of collaboration on a form-focused task. *Japanese Language Education around the Brobe, 6,* 101–123.

Hansen-Strain, L. (1993). The attrition of Japanese negation by English-speaking adults. Paper presented at the AILA - 10th World Congress of Applied Linguistics.

Harley, B. (1989). Functional grammar in French immersion : a classroom experiment. *Applied Linguistics, 10,* 331–59.

Harley, B. and Swain, M. (1984). The interlanguage of immersion students and its implications for second language teaching. In A. Davies, C. Criper and A. Howatt (Eds). *Interlanguage* (pp. 291–311). Edinburgh, Scotland: Edinburgh University Press.

Hatasa, A. Y. (2003). Studies on L2 writing instruction in the past and present. In Y. A. Hatasa (Ed.). *An Invitation to SLA Research* (pp. 207–218). Tokyo: Kurosio Publisher.

Hatasa, A. Y. and Soeda, E. (2001). Writing strategies revisited. A case of non-cognate L2 writers. In B. Swierzbin, F. Morris, M. E. Anderson, C. A. Klee and E. Tarone (Eds). *Social and Cognitive Factors in Second Language Acquisition. Selected Proceedings of the 1999 Second Language Research Forum* (pp. 375–396). Somerville, MA: Cascadilla Press.

Hatch, E. M. (1983). Simplified input and second language acquisition. In R.W. Andersen (Ed.). *Pidginization and Croelization as Language Acquisition* (pp. 64–86). Cambridge, MA: Newbury House.

Heikel, E. and Fotos, S. (Eds). (2002). *New Perspectives on Grammar Teaching in Second Language Classroom* . Mahwah, NJ: Lawrence Erlbaum Associates.

Hikima, N. (2009). Processing Instruction and Discourse in the acquisition of Japanese Passive Forms. In Benita, A. and and Lee, J. (2009). *Processing Instruction and Discourse* (pages forthcoming) London: Continuum.

Hulstijn, J. (1989). Implicit and incidental language learning: experiments in the processing of natural and partly artificial input. In H. Dechert and M. Raupach (Eds). *Interlingual Processes* (pp. 49–73). Tubingen: Gunter Narr.

Hymes, D. (1972). *On Communicative Competence.* In J. B. Pride and J. Holmes (Eds). *Sociolinguistics.* Harmondsworth, England: Penguin Books.

Inagaki, S. and Long, M. (1999). The effects of implicit negative feedback on the acquisition of Japanese as a second language. In K. Kanno (Ed.). *The Acquisition of Japanese as a Second Language* (pp. 35–52). Amsterdam: John Benjamins Publishing.

Iwashita, N. (1999). Tasks and learners' output in nonnative-nonnative interaction. In K. Kanno, (Ed.). *The Acquisition of Japanese as a Second Language* (pp. 53–70). Amsterdam: John Benjamins Publishing.

Iwashita, N. (2003). Negative feedback and positive evidence in task-based interaction: differential effects on L2 development. *Studies in Second Language Acquisition,* 25, 1–36.

Johnson, K. (1982). *Communicative Syllabus Design and Methodology.* London: Pergamon.

Kanagy, R. (1991). *Developmental Sequences in the Acquisition of Japanese as a Second Language: The Case of Negation.* Doctoral Thesis. University of Pennsylvania.

Kanagy, R. (1994). Developmental sequences in acquiring Japanese: negation in L1 and L2. In T. Fujimura, Y. Kato, M. Leoung and R. Uehara (Eds). *Proceedings of the 5th Conference on Second Language Research in Japan* (pp. 109–126). Niigata: International University of Japan.

Kanagy, R. (1999). Language socialization and affect in first and second language acquisition. Special Issue, *Journal of Pragmatics,* 31,11.

Kanno, K. (Ed.) (1999). *The Acquisition of Japanese as a Second Language.* Amsterdam: John Benjamins Publishing.

Kaplan, M. (1987). Developmental patterns of past tense acquisition among foreign language learners of French. In B. Van Patten, T. Dvorak and J. Lee (Eds). *Foreign Language Learning : A Research Perspective* (pp. 52–60). Rowley, MA: Newbury House.

Kawaguchi, S. (2005). Argument structure and syntactic development in Japanese as a second language. In M. Pienemann (Ed.). *Cross-Linguistic Aspects of Processability Theory* (pp. 253–298). New York: John Benjamins.

Kigawa, T. (1993). An analysis of composing strategies of Japanese learners. *Bulletin of Universities and Institutes* 6, 51–77.

Koyanagi, K., Maruishi, M., Muranos, H., Ota, M. and Shibata, N. (1994). Negative feedback and the acquisition of Japanese conditionals. Poster presented at the Second Language Research Forum. Montreal: McGill University.

Krashen, S. (1982). *Principles and Practice in Second Language Acquisition.* London: Pergamon.

Krashen, S. (1993). The Effects of Formal Grammar Teaching: Still Peripheral. *TESOL Quarterly,* 27, 22.

Kubota, S. (1999). Input enhancement: explicit vs. implicit types. *The Proceedings of the Seventh Princeton Japanese Pedagogy Workshop,* 122–145.

Larsen-Freeman, D. (1986). *Techniques and Principles in Language Teaching.* Oxford: OUP.

Larsen-Freeman, D. and Long, M. (1991). *An Introduction to Second Language Research.* New York: Longman.

Lee, J. (2000). *Tasks and Communicating in Language Classrooms.* New York: McGraw-Hill.

Lee, J. (2004). On the generalizability, limits, and potential future directions of processin instruction research. In B. Van Patten (Ed.). *Processing Instruction: Theory, Research and Commentary* (pp. 311–323). Mahwah, NJ: Lawrence Erlbaum Associates.

Lee, J. and Benati, A. G. *Grammar Acquisition and Processing Instruction.* Clevedon: Multilingual Matters.

Lee, J. F. and Benati, A. G. (2007a). *Delivering Processing Instruction in Classrooms and Virtual Contexts: Research and Practice.* London: Equinox.

Lee, J. F. and Benati, A. G. (2007b). *Second Language processing: An analysis of Theory, Problems and Possible Solutions.* London: Continuum.

Lee, J. and Van Patten, B. (1995). *Making Communicative Language Teaching Happen.* New York: McGraw-Hill.

Lee, J. and Van Patten, B. (2003). *Making Communicative Language Teaching Happen, 2nd ed.* New York: McGraw-Hill.

Lightbown, P. (1983). Exploring relationships between developmental and instructional sequences in L2 acquisition. In H. Seliger and M. Long (Eds). *Classroom Oriented Research in Language Acquisition.* Rowley, MA: Newbury House.

Lightbown, P. and Spada, N. (1990). Focus on form and corrective feedback in communicative language teaching: effects on second language learning. *Studies in Second Language Acquisition,* 12, 429–48.

Lightbown, P. and Spada, N. (1997). Learning English as a second language in a special school in Quebec. *Canadian Modern Language Review,* 53, 315–355.

Lightbown, P. and Spada, N. (1999). *How Languages Are Learned.* Oxford: OUP.

Littlewood, W. (1981). *Communicative Language Teaching.* Cambridge: CUP.

Littlewood, W. (1992). *Teaching Oral Communication.* Oxford: Blackwell.

Long, M. (1980). Inside the black box. Methodological issues in classroom research on language learning. *Language Learning*, 30, 1–42.

Long, M. (1983). Does second language instruction make a difference? *TESOL Quarterly*, 17, 359–82.

Long, M. (1984). Process and product in ESL program evaluation. *TESOL Quarterly*, 18, 409–425.

Long, M. (1991). Focus on form: a design feature in language teaching methodology. In K. De Bot, R. Ginsberg and C. Kramsch (Eds). Foreign Language Research in Cross-Cultural perspectives (pp. 39–52). *Amsterdam:* John Benjamins.

Long, M. (1996). The role of the linguistic environment in second language acquisition. In W. C. Ritchie and, T. K. Bhatia (Eds). *Handbook of second language acquisition* (pp. 413–68). San Diego, CA: Academic Press.

Long, M. and Robinson, P. (1998). Focus on form: theory, research and practice. In C. Doughty and J. Williams (Eds). *Focus on Form in Classroom Second Language Acquisition* (pp. 15–41). Cambridge: CUP.

Loschky, L. (1994). Comprehensible input and second language acquisition: what is the relationship? *Studies in Second Language Acquisition*, 16, 303–323.

Lyster, R. and Ranta, L. (1997). Corrective feedback and learner uptake: negotiation of form in communicative classrooms. *Studies in Second Language Acquisition*, 19, 37–66.

McLaughlin, B. (1978). The Monitor Model: some methodological considerations. *Language Learning*, 28, 309–332.

Mackey, A. (1995). Setting up the Pace: Input, Interaction and Interlanguage Development. An Empirical study of acquisition in ESL. Unpublished Doctoral dissertation. University of Sydney.

Mackey, A. and Gass, S. M. (2005). *Second Language Research: Methodology and Design*. Mahwah, NJ: Lawrence Erlbaum Associates.

Minaminosono, H. (1997). A Survey on the Relationship between Strategy Use and Reading Comprehension: The Case of Reading Japanese as a Foreign Language. *Japanese Language Education Around the Globe*, 7.

Mitchell, R. (1988). *Communicative Language Teaching in Practice*. London: CILT.

Mito, K. (1993). The effects of modelling and recasting on the acquisition of L2 grammar rules. Unpublished manuscript , University of Hawaii at Manoa.

Moroishi, M. (1999). Explicit vs. implicit learning: acquisition of the Japanese conjectural auxiliaries under explicit and implicit conditions. In N. Jungheim and P. Robinson (Eds). *Pragmatics and Pedagogy: Proceedings of the 3rd Pacific Second Language Research Forum, Volume 2*. (pp. 217–230). Tokyo: PacSLRF.

Moroishi, M. (2001). Recasts and learner uptake in Japanese classroom discourse. In X. Bonch-Bruevich, W. J. Crawford, J. Hellermann, C. Higgins and H. Nguyen (Eds). *The Past, Present and Future of Second Language Research. Selected Proceedings of the 2000 Second Language Research Forum* (pp. 197–208). Somerville, MA: Cascadilla Press.

Moroishi (2003). The role of input and interaction in the acquisition of Japanese as a second/foreign language. In Y. A. Hatasa, (Ed.). *An Invitation to SLA Research*. Tokyo: Kurosio Publisher.

Nagata, N. (1998). Input vs. output practice in educational software for second language acquisition. *Language Learning and Technology*, 1, 23–40.

Nakakubo, T. (1997). The role of modification in listening comprehension-an empirical study for the development of listening materials. *Journal of Japanese Language Teaching*, 95, 13–24.

Nassaji, H. and Fotos, S. (2004). Current developments in research on the teaching of grammar. *Annual Review of Applied Linguistics*, 24, 126–145.

Newark, L. (1966). How not to interfere in language learning. *International Journal of American Linguistics*, 32, 77–87.

Nobuyoshi, J. and Ellis, R. (1993). Focused communication tasks and second language acquisition. *ELT Journal*, 47, 203–210.

Norris, J. M. and Ortega, L. (2000). Effectiveness of L2 instruction: a research synthesis and quantitative meta-analysis. *Language Learning*, 50, 41 7–528.

Nunan, D. (1989). *Understanding Language Classrooms: A Guide for Instructor Initiated Action*. New York: Prentice-Hall.

Nunan, D. (1992). *Research Methods in Language Learning*. Cambridge: CUP.

Nunan, D. (2001). *Second Language Teaching and Learning*. Boston, MA: Heinle & Heinle Publishers.

Ohta, J. (2001a). *Second Language Acquisition Processes in the Classroom: Learning Japanese*. Mahwah, NJ: Lawrence Erlbaum Associates.

Ohta, J. (2001b). Rethinking recasts: a learner-centred examination of corrective feedback in the Japanese classroom. In J. K. Hall and L. Verplaste (Eds). *The Construction of Second and Foreign Language Learning through Classroom Interaction*. Mahwah, NJ: Lawrence Erlbaum Associates.

Omaggio, Hadley, A. (2001). *Teaching Language in Context*, 3rd ed. Boston, MA: Heinle & Heinle.

Paulston, C. (1972). Structural patterns drills: a classification. In H. Allen & R. Campbell (Eds.), *Teaching English as a Second Language* (pp. 129–138). New York: McGraw-Hill.

Pica, T. (1983). Adult acquisition of English as a second language under different conditions of exposure. *Language Learning*, 33, 465–497.

Pica, T. (1992). The textual outcomes of native speaker-non-native speaker negotiation: what do they reveal about second language learning? In C. Kramsch and S. McConnell-Ginet (Eds). *Text and Context* (pp. 198–237). Cambridge, MA: Heath.

Pica, T. (1994). Questions from the classroom: research perspectives. *TESOL Quarterly*, 29, 49–79.

Pienemann, M. (1984). Psychological constraints on the teachability of languages. *Second Language Acquisition*, 6, 186–214.

Pienemann, M. (1987). Determining the influence of instruction on L2 speech processing. *Australian Review of Applied Linguistics*, 10, 83–113.

Pienemann, M. (1998). *Language Processing and L2 Development*. New York: John Benjamins.

Prabhu, N. (1987). *Second Language Pedagogy*. Oxford: OUP.

Richards, J. C. and Rodgers, T. S. (1986). *Approaches and Methods in Language Teaching*. Cambridge: CUP.

Robinson, P. (1995). Task complexity and second language narrative discourse. *Language Learning*, 45, 99–140.

Robinson, P. (1996). Learning simple and complex second language rules under implicit, incidental, rule-search and instructed conditions. *Studies in Second Language Acquisition*, 18, 27–68.

Robinson, P. (1997). Automaticity and generalizability of second language learning under implicit, incidental, enhanced and instructed conditions. *Studies in Second Language Acquisition,* 19, 233–247.

Rost, M. (1990). *Listening in Language Learning.* London: Longman.

Rumelhart, D. (1980). Schemata: The building blocks of cognition. In S. B. Bruce and W. Brewer (Eds). *Theoretical Issues in Reading Comprehension.* Hillsdale, NJ: Lawrence Erlbaum Associates.

Rutherford, W. (1987). *Second Language Grammar: Teaching and learning.* London: Longman.

Rutherford, W. and Sharwood-Smith, M. (1988). *Grammar and Second Language Teaching.* Rowley, MA: Newbury House.

Samimy, K. (1989). A comparative study of teaching Japanese in the audio-lingual method and the counseling-learning approach. *Modern Language Journal,* 73, 169–177.

Sanz, C. (Ed.) (2005). *Mind and Context in Adult Second Language Acquisition.* Washington, DC: Georgetown University Press.

Sato, K. and Kleinsasser, R. C. (1999). Communicative language teaching (CLT): practical understandings. *The Modern Language Journal,* 83, 494–517.

Savignon, S. (1972). *Communicative Competence: An Experiment in Foreign Language Teaching.* Philadelphia, PA: Center for Curriculum Development.

Savignon, S. (2005). *Communicative Competence: Theory and Classroom Practice.* New York: McGraw-Hill.

Schmidt, R. (1990). The role of consciousness in second language learning. *Applied Linguistics,* 11, 129–158.

Schmidt, R. (1994). Deconstructing consciousness in search of useful definitions for applied linguistics. *AILA Review,* 11, 11–26.

Seliger, H. and Shohany, E. (1989). *Second Language Research Methods.* Oxford: OUP.

Sharwood-Smith, M. (1986). Comprehension versus acquisition: two ways of processing input. *Applied Linguistics* 7, 239–274.

Sharwood-Smith, M. (1991). Speaking to many minds: on the relevance of different types of language information for the L2 learner. *Second Language Research* 7, 118–132.

Sharwood-Smith, M. (1993). Input enhancement in instructed SLA: theoretical bases. *Studies in Second Language Acquisition* 15, 165–179.

Sherer, A. and Wertheimer, M. (1964). *A Psycholinguistic Experiment in Foreign Language Teaching.* New York: McGraw Hill.

Skehan, P. (1996). A framework for the implementation of task-based instruction. *Applied Linguistics,* 17, 38–62.

Spada, N. (1987). Relationship between instructional differences and learning outcomes: a process-product study of communicative language teaching. *Applied Linguistics,* 8, 137–161.

Spada, N. (1990). A look at the research process in the classroom observation: a case study. In C. Brumfit and R. Mitchell (Eds). *Research in the Language Classroom* London: Modern English Publications.

Spada, N. (1997). Form-focused instruction and second language acquisition : a review of classroom and laboratory research. *LanguageTeaching* 30, 73–87.

Spada, N. and Lightbown, P. (1993). Instruction and the development of questions in L2 classrooms. *Studies in Second Language Acquisition,* 15, 205–224.

Swain, M. (1985). Communicative competence: some roles of comprehensible input and comprehensible output in its development. In S. Gass and C. Madden (Eds). *Input in Second Language Acquisition* (pp. 235–253). Rowley, MA: Newbury House.

Swain, M. (1995). Three functions of output in second language learning. In G. Cook and B. Seidlhofer (Eds). *Principles and Practice in the Study of Language.* Oxford: OUP.

Takashima, H. and Sugiura, R. (2006). Integration of theory and practice in grammar teaching: grammaring, grammarization and task activities. In A. Yoshitomi, T. Umino, and M. Negishi (Eds). *Readings in Second Language Pedagogy and Second Language Acquisition* (pp. 59–74). New York: John Benjamins.

Terrell, T. D. (1986). Acquisition in the natural approach: the binding\access framework. *The Modern Language Journal,* 70, 213–228.

Terrell, T. (1977). A natural approach to second language acquisition and learning. *The Modern Language Journal,* 61, 325.

Terrell, T. D. (1991). The role of grammar instruction in a communicative approach. *The Modern Language Journal,* 75, 52–63.

Trahey, M. and White, L. (1993). Positive evidence and preemption in the second language classroom. *Studies in Second Language Acquisition,* 15, 181–204.

Van Lier, L. (1988). *The Classroom and the Language Learner: ethnography and second language acquisition.* London: Longman.

Van Patten, B. (1999). What is Second Language Acquisition and What is it doing in my Department? *ADFL Bulletin,* 30.

Van Patten, B., Williams, J., Rott, S. and Overstreet, M. (2004). *Form-Meaning Connections in Second Language Acquisition.* Mahwah NJ: Lawrence Erlbaum Associates.

Van Patten, B. (1990). Attending to content and form in the input: an experiment in consciousness. *Studies in Second Language Acquisition* 12, 287–301.

Van Patten, B. (1996). *Input Processing and Grammar Instruction: Theory and Research.* Norwood, NJ: Ablex.

Van Patten, B. (2000). Processing instruction as form-meaning connections: issues in theory and research. In J. F. Lee and A. Valdman (Eds). *Form and Meaning: Multiple Perspectives* (pp. 43–68). Boston, MA: Heinle & Heinle.

Van Patten, B. (2002). Processing instruction: an update. *Language Learning* 52, 755–803.

Van Patten, B. (2003). *From Input to Output: A Teacher's Guide to Second Language Acquisition.* New York: McGraw-Hill.

Van Patten, B. (Ed.). (2004). *Processing Instruction: Theory, Research, and Commentary.* Mahwah, NJ: Lawrence Erlbaum Associates.

Van Patten, B. and Cadierno, T. (1993). Explicit instruction and input processing. *Studies in Second Language Acquisition,* 15, 225–243.

Van Patten, B. and Oikennon, S. (1996). Explanation vs. structured input in processing instruction. *Studies in Second Language Acquisition,* 18, 495–510.

Van Patten, B. and Williams, J. (2007). *Theories in SLA*. Mahwah, NJ: Lawrence Erlbaum Associates.

Van Patten, B. and Wong, W. (2004). Processing instruction and the French causative: another replication. In B. Van Patten (Ed.), *Processing Instruction: Theory, Research and Commentary* (pp. 97–118). Mahwah, NJ: Lawrence Erlbaum Associates.

Van Patten, B. and Mandell, P. B. (1999). Variable performance on grammaticality judgment tests: the role of knowledge source. Unpublished manuscript.

White, L. (1987). Against comprehensible input: the Input Hypothesis and the development of L2 competence. *Applied Linguistics*, 8, 95–110.

White, L. (1991). Adverb placement in SLA: some effects of positive and negative evidence in the classroom. *Second Language Research*, 7, 133–61.

White, L. (2003). *Second Language Acquisition and Universal Grammar*. Cambridge: CUP.

Widdowson, H. (1990). Aspects of Language Teaching. Oxford: OUP.

Wilkins, D. (1974). *Second Language Learning and Teaching*. London: Edward Arnold.

Wilkins, D. (1976). *Notional Syllabuses: A Taxonomy and its Relevance to Foreign Language Curriculum Development*. London: OUP.

Williams, J. and Evans, J. (1998). What kind of focus and on which forms? In C. Doughty and J. Williams (Eds.). *Focus on Form in Second Language Classroom Acquisition*. (pp. 139–155). Cambridge, MA: CUP.

Wolwin, A. and Coakley, C. (1985). *Listening Brown*. Oxford: OUP.

Wong, W. (2004a). The nature of processing instruction. In B. Van Patten (Ed.). *Processing Instruction: Theory, Research and Commentary* (pp. 33–63). Mahwah, NJ: Lawrence Erlbaum Associates.

Wong. W. (2004b). Processing instruction in French: the roles of explicit information and structured input. In B. Van Patten (Ed.). *Processing Instruction: Theory, Research and Commentary* (pp. 187–205). Mahwah, NJ: Lawrence Erlbaum Associates.

Wong, W. (2005). *Input Enhancement: From Theory and Research to the Classroom*. New York: McGraw-Hill.

Wong, W. and Van Patten, B. (2003). The evidence is IN: drills are OUT. *Foreign Language Annals* 36, 403–423.

Author Index

Subject Index